Pocket
MARRAKESH
TOP SIGHTS · LOCAL LIFE · MADE EASY

D0047000

Jessica Lee

In This Book

QuickStart Guide

Your keys to understanding the city – we help you decide what to do and how to do it

Need to Know
Tips for a smooth trip

Neighbourhoods
What's where

Explore Marrakesh

The best things to see and do, neighbourhood by neighbourhood

Top Sights
Make the most of your visit

Local Life
The insider's city

The Best of Marrakesh

The city's highlights in handy lists to help you plan

Best Walks
See the city on foot

Marrakesh's Best...
The best experiences

Survival Guide

Tips and tricks for a seamless, hassle-free city experience

Getting Around
Travel like a local

Essential Information
Including where to stay

Our selection of the city's best places to eat, drink and experience:

⊙ **Sights**

✖ **Eating**

☻ **Drinking**

✪ **Entertainment**

🔒 **Shopping**

These symbols give you the vital information for each listing:

☏ Telephone Numbers	👪 Family-Friendly
⊙ Opening Hours	🐾 Pet-Friendly
P Parking	🚌 Bus
⊖ Nonsmoking	🛳 Ferry
@ Internet Access	M Metro
📶 Wi-Fi Access	S Subway
🥗 Vegetarian Selection	🚋 Tram
📖 English-Language Menu	🚆 Train

Find each listing quickly on maps for each neighbourhood:

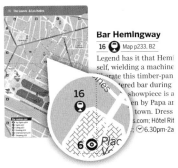

The Louvre & Les Halles

Bar Hemingway

16 ☻ Map p233, B2

Legend has it that Hemi self, wielding a machine rate this timber-pan ered bar during showpiece is a en by Papa ar town. Dress s.com; Hôtel Rit ⊙6.30pm-2a

Lonely Planet's Marrakesh

Lonely Planet Pocket Guides are designed to get you straight to the heart of the city.

Inside you'll find all the must-see sights, plus tips to make your visit to each one really memorable. We've split the city into easy-to-navigate neighbourhoods and provided clear maps so you'll find your way around with ease. Our expert authors have searched out the best of the city: walks, food, nightlife and shopping, to name a few. Because you want to explore, our 'Local Life' pages will take you to some of the most exciting areas to experience the real Marrakesh.

And of course you'll find all the practical tips you need for a smooth trip: itineraries for short visits, how to get around, and how much to tip the guy who serves you a drink at the end of a long day's exploration.

It's your guarantee of a really great experience.

Our Promise

You can trust our travel information because Lonely Planet authors visit the places we write about, each and every edition. We never accept freebies for positive coverage, so you can rely on us to tell it like it is.

The Best of Marrakesh **121**

Survival Guide **143**

QuickStart Guide

Welcome to Marrakesh

Prepare for your senses to be slapped awake. Storytellers, snail-vendors and conjurors collide on Djemaa el-Fna, from where ochre-dusted lanes lead to intriguing souqs. While the thriving art scene and cafe culture generate a cosmopolitan buzz, it's the medina's heady scents and sounds that bedazzle, frazzle and enchant. Put on your pointy *babouches* (leather slippers) and dive in.

Djemaa el-Fna (p24) at dusk
FRANS LEMMENS/GETTY IMAGES ©

Marrakesh Top Sights

Djemaa el-Fna (p24)

Marrakesh's madcap main plaza revs into gear every evening as the sun sets for a night of hoopla, *halqa* (street theatre) and *hikayat* (storytelling). The only option is to join in.

IZZET KERIBAR/GETTY IMAGES ©

HUW JONES/GETTY IMAGES ©

Ali ben Youssef Medersa (p60)

The artistry of Islamic architecture reaches its epoch in the courtyard of this old *medersa* (theological college), a masterpiece of arabesque design.

Bahia Palace (p82)

Inside this prime piece of medina real estate, tranquil inner courtyards lead onto salons where Marrakshi artisans went to town in a frenzy of *zellij* (ceramic tile mosaic) and *zouak* (painted wood).

Saadian Tombs (p84)

Sultan Ahmed al-Mansour ed-Dahbi knew how to make a statement, and his sumptuous mausoleum is a fittingly exuberant exclamation mark to finish off the Saadian era's might.

Jardin Majorelle (p102)

Come here to stroll the colourful and quirky botanical garden, famously once owned by fashion mogul Yves Saint Laurent, and to view the dazzling artefact collection inside the Berber Museum.

Maison de la Photographie (p64)

View Moroccan lifestyles and landscapes as captured through the early camera lens. The superb collection of vintage photography here unveils a vision of Morocco now consigned to history.

Dar Si Said (p86)

Moroccan craft abounds in this medina mansion. While the ground floor is home to the exhibits of the Museum of Moroccan Art collection, the *zouak* ceilings upstairs are the real show-stopper.

Musée de Marrakech (p62)

Marrakesh high society sure knew how to live it up in the 19th century. This former palace's inner courtyard is a vision of *zellij* and intricate carved wood fit for a pasha.

Koutoubia Mosque (p26)

Guarding the entry to the medina since the Almohad age, the gold-hued stone minaret of the Koutoubia Mosque remains Marrakesh's most distinct and famous landmark.

Palmeraie (p118)

When the heat valve gets turned up full-throttle, the shaded palm groves on the city's edge, with camel-ride and quad-biking opportunities, provide welcome relief.

Marrakesh Local Life

Insider tips to help you find the real city

Marrakesh has always been more about ambience than a mere list of sights to tick off. Delve into the narrow lanes of the medina to explore how Marrakshis are merging modern life with ancient traditions.

Chic Souqs (p54)

▶ Funky boutiques
▶ Marrakshi designers

Traditional market streets get a modern overhaul in Mouassine, where local young designers are trailblazing a contemporary scene. Proof that Marrakesh is no stale museum piece but instead a thriving centre of artistry moving with the times.

Bab Doukkala Neighbourhood Stroll (p44)

▶ Quiet back lanes
▶ Residential life

Wander away from the main souqs and you'll find the spindling *derbs* (alleys) where Marrakshis live without a trinket shop in sight.

The Heart of the Souqs (p67)

▶ Artisan workshops
▶ Local markets

Marrakesh's core of commerce offers more than Souq Semmarine and Souq el-Kebir. Meander through Souq Haddadine (Blacksmith's Souq) and explore the confines of the *qissariat* (covered markets) to discover the life behind the souvenir stalls.

Exploring Around Bab Debbagh (p68)

▶ Tanneries
▶ Marabout shrine

Stroll through the northeast slice of the medina where tanners continue their back-breaking trade and *marabouts* (saints) are still venerated at local pilgrimage shrines. This corner of the old town exposes the time-honoured traditions still playing a role in modern Marrakshi life.

Guéliz Gallery Hop (p104)

▶ Art galleries
▶ Cafe culture

Head to Guéliz in the Ville Nouvelle (new town) for a completely different take on Marrakesh's cultural life. This is the hub of the city's growing contemporary-art scene, with a clutch of art galleries and a thriving cafe culture to explore.

Tannery worker, Bab Debbagh (p68)

Lantern shopping in one of Marrakesh's souqs (p66)

Other great places to experience the city as a local:

Amal Centre (p111)

Haj Mustapha (p32)

Souq Ablueh (p31)

Hammam Dar el-Bacha (p50)

Mellah Market (p98)

Plats Haj Boujemaa (p111)

Rue ibn Aicha (p112)

Rue de la Kasbah (p94)

Oscar Progrès (p32)

Marrakesh Day Planner

Day One

Spend the morning diving into the **central souqs** (p58) before they get swamped with crowds. Sniff out spice at **Place Rahba Kedima** and stop for a mid-morning mint-tea break at **Café des Épices** (p74). Afterwards experience a double whammy of architectural glory at the **Ali ben Youssef Medersa** (p60) and the **Musée de Marrakech** (p62).

Head down to the Djemaa for lunch at **Mechoui Alley** (p29) to munch on slow-roasted lamb the Moroccan way. Then embrace historic finery viewing the glorious ceilings of **Bahia Palace** (p82) and the dazzling **Saadian Tombs** (p84). Treat yourself to a luxe ice cream at **Panna Gelato** (p94) as you wander back into the medina's central hub, stopping off to view the graceful interiors and exhibits of the **Dar Si Said** (p86) on the way.

Grab a spot on one of the rooftop terraces of **Djemaa el-Fna** (p24) as the **Koutoubia Mosque's** (p26) floodlights are turned on and then wander through the square as the musicians strike up for the night. Duck away from the plaza for gourmet feasting at **Le Tobsil** (p33) but stroll back afterwards to experience the best of the late-night carnival action.

Day Two

A morning in **Mouassine** (p52) beckons. Check out Marrakesh's caravan history in **Funduq el-Amir** (p47) then admire the restored finery on show at the **Musée Douiria de Mouassine** (p47). Trawl for original gift ideas amid the funky boutiques of **Souk Cherifa** (p43), spot textile dyers at work in **Souq Sebbaghine** then pop your feet up in leafy **Le Jardin** (p51) for a relaxed lunch.

Weave your way through the narrow alleys to see the blacksmiths hammering away in **Souq Haddadine** before viewing a slice of old Marrakesh in **Maison de la Photographie** (p64). Stop off at **Musée Boucharouite** (p71) for a peek at lesser-known Moroccan crafts then scrub off the souq dust and rejuvenate aching joints with a hammam at **Le Bain Bleu** (p48).

When you're steamed and scrubbed to a rosy pink glow, head to **Café Arabe** (p53) for a sunset drink or two, then get ready for top-notch tajine action at **Al-Fassia** (p110) in the Ville Nouvelle. If you're in the mood to sample a slice of Guéliz nightlife afterwards, check out **Café du Livre** (p112) for a cocktail in its cosy bar.

Short on time?
We've arranged Marrakesh's must-sees into these day-by-day itineraries to make sure you see the very best of the city in the time you have available.

Day Three

Grab a coffee at **Café 16** (p105) then pop into the **Matisse Art Gallery** (p104) to view Moroccan art both old and new. Continue on arty ground with a stroll through the old painter abode of **Jardin Majorelle** (p102). Wrap yourself up in this tranquil haven of bamboo groves, birdsong and lashings of cobalt blue and brush up on Berber culture within the garden's fabulous **Berber Museum**.

Dig into lunch for a good cause at the friendly **Amal Centre** (p111), where Moroccan home cooking is at the menu's fore. Then head to the kasbah for an afternoon getting lost amid the skinny alleyways of the **mellah** (Jewish quarter) before visiting **Maison Tiskiwin** (p90) to view the ethnographic exhibits. Sit upon the ramparts surveying the ruins and their noisy storks in **Badi Palace** (p89) then hop across to **Kosybar** (p97) for a well-earned drink and more stork-watching on the rooftop.

Go local for dinner at one of the grill restaurants on **Rue de la Kasbah**, then head to **Cafe Clock** (p94) to check out what live music or cultural event it has on its calendar that night.

Day Four

Discover some quieter medina action amid the *derbs* (alleys) that spiral off **Rue Bab Doukkala** before dropping into **Henna Cafe** (p45) for a mint-tea break and maybe a bit of henna art on your hands. Pick up souvenirs with feel-good factor at the friendly cooperative shops of **Al Kawtar** (p56) and **Al Nour** (p37), slather yourself in argan products at **Assouss Cooperative d'Argane** (p42) and maybe invest in a treat or two from **Anamil** (p77).

Shopping over for the day, experience a slice of chic Marrakesh in the afternoon with a chill-out lazy lunch and some serious poolside lounging amid the palm-shaded haven of **Le Jardins de la Medina** (p91). A bit of swimming and sunbathing is the perfect antidote for souq-weary feet.

After all that relaxation it's time to dive full throttle back into Marrakesh life by sampling some more of the magic of **Djemaa el-Fna** (p24). Snack on snails (if you dare), watch music troupes and acrobats woo the punters, grab a bite to eat at a Djemaa food stall and soak up the full-on craziness of the open-air theatre for one last time.

Need to Know

**For more information,
see Survival Guide (p143)**

....

Currency

Moroccan dirham (Dh)

....

Language

Moroccan Arabic (Darija), Berber, French

....

Visas

Most visitors do not require a visa and are
allowed to remain in Morocco for 90 days
on entry.

....

Money

ATMs are widely available. Credit cards are
commonly accepted in midrange and top-
end hotels and restaurants as well as large
tourist-oriented shops.

....

Mobile Phones

Local SIM cards are cheap and can be used
in any unlocked phone. Bring your passport
when purchasing a SIM card.

....

Time

Western European Time
(same as GMT/UTC)

....

Plugs & Adaptors

Plugs have European-style two round pins;
electrical current is 220V.

....

Tipping

Baksheesh (tipping) is an integral part of
Moroccan life. Tip 10% at restaurants; Dh3–5
for porters and baggage handlers; and Dh2 to
public-toilet attendants.

....

❶ Before You Go

Your Daily Budget

Budget less than Dh500

► Budget double room Dh100–Dh350

► Cheap museum-entrance fees (Dh10–Dh40)

► Free evening entertainment at Djemaa
el-Fna (don't forget to tip!)

Midrange Dh750–Dh1000

► Riad double room Dh350–Dh750

► Three-course lunch set menu Dh120–
Dh170

► Private hammam soak and scrub from
Dh250

Top end over Dh1400

► Boutique-riad double room from Dh800

► Dinner in riad-style restaurant Dh250–
Dh500

► Cocktail at bar Dh80–Dh100

Useful Websites

Maroc Mama (http://marocmama.com) Marrakesh food and travel blog.

Lonely Planet (www.lonelyplanet.com/mar-
rakesh) Information, bookings and forums.

Marrakech Pocket (www.marrakechpocket.
com) Monthly 'What's On?' guide.

Advance Planning

Two months before Book riad accommodation; particularly important if travelling in
high season.

One month before Organise activities
such as cooking classes (most have limited
spaces).

One day before Check the weather. Marrakesh gets colder than you think in winter,
and fiercely hot in summer.

② Arriving in Marrakesh

Menara Airport is 6km southwest of town. Marrakesh's train station is conveniently located in the Ville Nouvelle; check schedules on **Marrakech Train Tickets** (www.marrakechtraintickets.com). Most buses arrive at the CTM bus station, southwest from the train station.

✈ From Menara Airport

Destination	Best Transport
Central Souqs area	Airport transfer pre-arranged through hotel
Djemaa el-Fna	Petit taxi (local taxi) or airport bus 19
Palmeraie	Airport transfer or petit taxi (local taxi)
Ville Nouville	Petit taxi (local taxi)

✈ At the Airport

Menara Airport The arrivals hall has currency exchange, ATMs and a tourist-information desk. The taxi rank is directly outside the terminal. Cross over the car park to pick up a taxi that will quote a lower fare. Airport bus 19 (every half-hour) runs from outside the airport car park.

Note when departing Marrakesh, all duty-free shops and most other services in the departure lounge after immigration only accept euros.

③ Getting Around

Most of the medina is a no-car zone so you need to get your walking shoes on to properly explore the lanes of Marrakesh's old city. If the weather is not too hot it's a straightforward 20 to 25 minute stroll from Djemaa el-Fna up Ave Mohammed V to the Ville Nouvelle. At other times, plenty of taxis and local buses ply this route.

🚗 Taxi

Creamy-beige petits taxis around town should charge Dh8 to Dh20 per journey, with a Dh10 surcharge at night. Meters are supposed to be used but are often not. No trip within town should cost more than Dh20 by day and Dh30 at night.

Most drivers at taxi ranks near popular tourist locations such as Djemaa el-Fna and Jardin Majorelle quote exorbitant fees. Hail off the street for better rates. If your party numbers more than three you must take a grand taxi (shared taxi), which always requires negotiation.

🚌 Bus

A variety of local buses zip between stops near Place de Foucauld (by Djemaa el-Fna) and the Ville Nouvelle at regular intervals throughout the day. All fares are Dh4.

Calèches

These horse-drawn carriages provide a scenic and relaxed option for journeys between Djemaa el-Fna and Jardin Majorelle and the Djemaa to the sights in the kasbah. Standard prices for routes and hourly fees should be listed on each carriage.

Marrakesh Neighbourhoods

Jardin Majorelle

Ville Nouvelle (p100)

Modern Marrakesh offers art galleries, top restaurants and shady parks to escape the hurly-burly of the medina.

◉ Top Sights

Jardin Majorelle

Djemaa el-Fna & Around (p22)

Marrakesh's main square is where carnival and cultural hub collide. Atmospheric and a touch chaotic, this is the city's heart.

◉ Top Sights

Djemaa el-Fna

Koutoubia Mosque

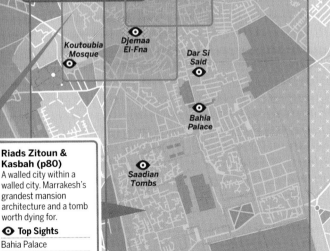

Mouassine & Bab Doukkala (p40)
Funky boutiques and handicraft stores sit side by side in this medina neighbourhood of narrow passageways and blush-pink walls.

Worth a Trip
◉ Top Sights
Palmeraie

Central Souqs (p58)
Shop-til-you-drop souqs full of lively hustle and bustle and a magnificent *medersa*.
◉ Top Sights
Ali ben Youssef Medersa
Musée de Marrakech
Maison de la Photographie

Ali ben Youssef Medersa ◉
Musée de Marrakech ◉
◉ Maison de la Photographie

Koutoubia Mosque ◉

Djemaa El-Fna ◉

Dar Si Said ◉

◉ Bahia Palace

Riads Zitoun & Kasbah (p80)
A walled city within a walled city. Marrakesh's grandest mansion architecture and a tomb worth dying for.
◉ Top Sights
Bahia Palace
Saadian Tombs
Dar Si Said

◉ Saadian Tombs

Explore
Marrakesh

Colourful goods line Marrakesh's souqs
GAVIN HELLIER/GETTY IMAGES ©

Explore

Djemaa el-Fna & Around

Dorothy and Toto had their Oz, Alice had her wonderland and now you can experience the out-of-this-world pandemonium that is Djemaa el-Fna. This crazy, chaotic hub is the heart and soul of Marrakesh, where snakes are charmed by day, music troupes shimmy and shake at night and visitors look on wide-eyed. Prepare to be swept up into the mayhem.

VISIONS OF OUR LAND/GETTY IMAGES ©

The Sights in a Day

☀ Say good morning to the minaret of the **Koutoubia Mosque** (p26) and do a circle of the grounds to check out the excavation site. Head to **Pâtisserie des Princes** (p29) for coffee and *pain au chocolat* then stroll across near-empty **Djemaa el-Fna** (p24) to see the square in its rare quiet moments.

☀ Spend the afternoon mooching through the nearby souqs to get a feel for what's on offer. Check out **Al Nour** (p37) for beautiful souvenirs supporting a worthy cause, and the cupboard-sized jewellery stores of **Funduq el Ouarzazi** (p37) for Berber designs and Tuareg symbols. Sample lunch local-style with the Marrakshi speciality of *tanjia* (slow-cooked stew) at **Haj Mustapha** (p32).

☾ In the early evening head back to the **Djemaa** to watch the food stands set up for the night as the crowds start to stream in. Hunt out storytellers between 4pm and 8pm when they're most likely to be performing and then flit between huddled groups to see what's entertaining them. Sit down at the food stalls for dinner when you start suffering sensory-overload.

◉ Top Sights

Djemaa el-Fna (p24)

Koutoubia Mosque (p26)

♥ Best of Marrakesh

Food

Le Tobsil (p33)

Gastro MK (p33)

Mechoui Alley (p29)

Haj Mustapha (p32)

Pâtisserie des Princes (p29)

Shopping

Al Nour (p37)

Funduq el Ouarzazi (p37)

Clubs & Bars

Piano Bar (p34)

Getting There

🚌 **Bus** Buses 1, 8, 10, 14 and 66 head from the Ville Nouvelle via Bab Doukkala to stops at Pl de Foucauld, right next to Djemaa el-Fna.

🚖 **Taxi** Taxis usually drop passengers either near the post office (right on Djemaa el-Fna) or at the taxi rank opposite the Koutoubia Mosque, beside Pl de Foucauld.

Top Sights
Djemaa el-Fna

Think of it as live-action channel surfing: everywhere you look in Djemaa el-Fna, Marrakesh's main square, you'll discover drama in progress. The hoopla and *halqa* (street theatre) has been nonstop here ever since this plaza was the site of public executions around AD 1050 – hence its name, which means 'assembly of the dead'.

By 10am the daily performance is already underway but as the shadows fall the circus revs up and acrobats, storytellers and musicians keep the Djemaa pumping until late.

Map p28, D2

⊘shows approx 9am-1am, later during Ramadan

Food stall, Djemaa el-Fna

Don't Miss

Morning Quiet

Stroll the Djemaa as it wakes up for the day to catch the plaza at its least frenetic. The orange-juice vendors have arrived, water sellers in fringed hats begin clanging brass cups together and the earliest of the potion sellers and henna-tattoo artists start setting up makeshift stalls under sunshades.

Lull Before the Storm

Djemaa's storytellers get going by mid-afternoon and recite ancient epics long into the evening. While you're weaving your way across the square looking out for these renowned yarn-spinners, an acrobat may cartwheel past and a man sporting fairy wings and walking a tutu-clad monkey will probably stroll on by. The Djemaa is finding its daily mojo.

Dinner at Djemaa

Pull up a pew at one of the Djemma el-Fna food stalls to score ringside seats on the action. Chefs set up shop just before dusk and woo customers in with grilled meats, tajines and more adventurous Marrakesh specialities such as snail soup, sheep's brain and skewered hearts. Now that's a meal to write home about.

The Carnival

Roll up, for the greatest show on earth. At sunset the musicians start tuning up and locals flood into the square. Squeeze between clowns and cross-dressing bellydancers, pause at a boxing match and tap your toes to the music of the Gnaoua troupes. The Djemaa doesn't knock off for the night until around 1am.

☑ Top Tips

▶ Keep a stock of Dh1 coins on hand. You'll need them for tipping the performers. A few dirhams is all that's necessary when the hat comes around.

▶ Arrive early in the evening to nab prime seats on makeshift stools (women and elders get preference).

▶ Despite alarmist warnings, your stomach should be fine eating at the Djemaa night stalls. Clean your hands before eating, use your bread instead of rinsed utensils and stick to your own bottled water.

▶ Stay alert to horse-drawn-carriage traffic, pickpockets and rogue gropers.

✕ Take a Break

If you feel your energy flagging head to the terrace of **Café Kes-sabine** (p32) for a mint tea, or follow your nose to **Mechoui Alley** (p29) where the stalls dish up succulent *mechoui* (slow-roasted lamb).

Top Sights
Koutoubia Mosque

Five times a day the voice of the Koutoubia's muezzin rises above the Djemaa din, calling the faithful to prayer. The Koutoubia Mosque's minaret has been standing guard over the old city since the Almohads raised it in the 12th century. Once 100 booksellers clustered around its base – hence the mosque's name, from *kutubiyyin* (booksellers). Today it is Marrakesh's most famous landmark. Gaze up at the ornate decoration and marvel at the masonic mastery of the minaret's Almohad-era builders.

◉ Map p28, A4

cnr Rue el-Koutoubia & Ave Mohammed V

⊘mosque & minaret closed to non-Muslims, gardens open 8am-8pm

Koutoubia Mosque's minaret stands tall over the old city

Don't Miss

Crenellations to Inspire Copycats

They say imitation is the greatest compliment and this 70m-high tower has quite the reputation as an architectural muse. It's the prototype for Seville's La Giralda and Rabat's Le Tour Hassan, as well as being a monumental cheat sheet of Moorish ornamentation. Crane your neck to check out the scalloped keystone arches and jagged *merlons* (crenellations).

Golden-Stoned Beauty

Marrakesh's other medina mosques are covered in a layer of pink plaster and originally the Koutoubia would have been decorated like this as well. After the minaret's restoration in the 1990s, city authorities decided to maintain the minaret's natural golden-hued stone, a decision that allows the Koutoubia to stand out dramatically amid the old city's candy-tinted tones.

Legends of the Spire

The minaret is topped by a spire of copper balls, sticking up antenna-like and glinting in the sun. Once made from gold, local legend tells that the balls were 'gifted' to the mosque by the wife of Almohad Sultan Yacoub el-Mansour, who melted down her jewellery as punishment after being spotted eating during Ramadan fasting hours.

Excavation Area

On the northwest side of the minaret are the ruins of the first mosque built on this spot, revealed by excavation work. This original mosque hadn't been properly aligned with Mecca, so the pious Almohads insisted on building a realigned one right next door. Walk behind the ruins for the best view of the excavation site.

☑ Top Tips

▶ Non-Muslims can't actually enter the mosque or minaret but you'll get great views of the minaret's stunning architecture from all angles by walking a full circuit around the complex, starting from the esplanade in front.

▶ Come once during the day to photograph the minaret against a backdrop of blue sky, and then again just after sunset when the minaret's floodlights have been turned on.

▶ If you're feeling frazzled by all the Djemaa el-Fna action, the palm tree-studded Koutoubia Gardens directly behind the mosque are a soothing respite.

✕ Take a Break

Refuel with a sugar fix at **Pâtisserie des Princes** (p29), lauded for its pastries. For a quick drink, head across the road to **Café L'Arôme** (p36) for for a coffee while you admire the minaret from a distance.

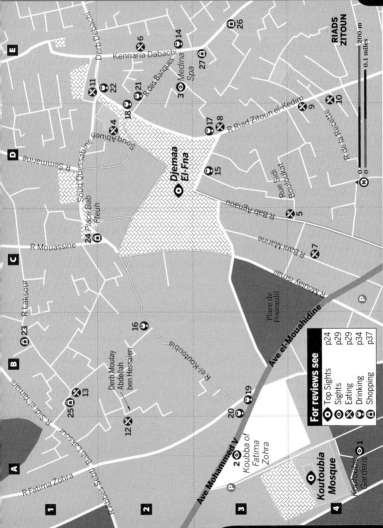

RIADS
ZITOUN

200 m
0.1 miles

Derb Dabachi

26

6

14

Kennaria Dabachi

27

11

22

21

R des Banques

3 Medina
Spa

18

4

Souq Ableuh

17

8

R Riad Zitoun el-Kedim

9

10

R de la Recette

Souq Quessabine

R Semmarine

Djemaa
El-Fna

15

Rue Sidi
Boulokat

R Bab Arnaou

24 Place Bab
Fteuh

R Mouassine

5

R Bani Marine

R Moulay Ismail

7

R Laksour

Place de
Fouetild

23

R el-Koutoubia

16

Ave el-Mouahidine

Derb Moulay
Abdellah
ben Hessaien

R Sidi el-Kramli

13

25

12

19

20

2

Koubba of
Fatima
Zohra

Ave Mohammed V

Koutoubia
Mosque

R Sidi Laksour

R Bab Laksour

Bab-Sedri

R Fatima Zohra

Koutoubia
Gardens

1

For reviews see

◆ Top Sights	p24
◉ Sights	p29
✕ Eating	p29
🍷 Drinking	p34
🛍 Shopping	p37

Sights

Koutoubia Gardens PARK

1 Map p28, A4

Stretching out behind the Koutoubia
Mosque, this palm tree-dotted swath
of greenery is a Marrakshi favourite
spot for strolling, relaxing on park
benches and generally taking a quiet
break. If you need some downtime
after dodging motorbikes amid the
medina's skinny alleyways, take the
locals' lead and head here for a peaceful meander. There are great views of
the Koutoubia Mosque's minaret from
here as well. (Ave Mohammed V)

Koubba of Fatima Zohra TOMB

2 Map p28, A3

This plain white and modest structure
is the tomb of Fatima Zohra, daughter
of a revered local religious leader. Local
legends abound about Fatima Zohra's
mystical powers but the most popular
story is that she would turn into a dove
every evening and only resume human
form at sunrise. (Ave Mohammed V)

Medina Spa HAMMAM

3 Map p28, E2

Steps from the dusty Djemaa, off Rue
des Banques, enjoy a brisk scrubbing
and rejuvenating massage. This is a
busy riad-spa, so expect some noise
and waits for walk-ins. (✆0524 38 50
59; www.medina-spa-marrakech.com; 27
Derb Zaari; scrub & massage package Dh325;
⏰9.30am-9pm)

☑ Top Tip

Getting Cash in the Medina

No, you don't need to troop all the
way to the Ville Nouvelle to find
an ATM (guichets automatiques).
There are ATMs on Rue Bab
Agnaou (which runs off Djemaa
el-Fna) and also near Pl Rahba
Kedima. Time your cashflow so you
don't need to top up your funds on
a Sunday when the medina ATMs
tend to be empty of cash.

Eating

Mechoui Alley MOROCCAN $

4 🍴 Map p28, D2

Just before noon, the vendors at this
row of stalls start carving up steam-
ing sides of mechoui (slow-roasted
lamb). Point to the best-looking cut
of meat, and ask for a nuss (half) or
rubb (quarter) kilo. The cook will hack
off falling-from-the-bone lamb and
hand it to you with fresh-baked bread,
cumin, salt and olives. (Souq Ablueh, east
side; meals Dh50-70; ⏰11am-2pm)

Pâtisserie des Princes PATISSERIE $

5 🍴 Map p28, C4

This is one of the city's most famous
patisseries, with enough pain au
chocolat, petit fours, almond cookies
and ice cream to keep Djemaa el-Fna
dentists in business. The small cafe
at the back is a welcome respite for
women, or anyone in search of a quiet

Understand
Storytellers and Tall Tales

The Original Smooth Talkers

Morocco has a strong tradition of *hikayat* (oral storytelling). For centuries, history soaked in myth, as well as fictional ancient epics of heroic derring-do and morality tales, have been passed down through the generations by storytellers whose narrative skills were highly prized and sought after.

This popular art form was not just for entertainment. It was a vital tool for passing on knowledge about the wider world. Storytellers regaled eager listeners with tales from the great Arab classic *The Thousand and One Nights*, narrated the lives of *marabouts* (saints), spun Moroccan folk tales and fables and told wondrous and terrible stories of faraway travel and adventure.

Djemaa el-Fna is thought to have been firmly established as a central platform for storytellers to wow the crowds by the 11th century. It is because of this age-old tradition that Unesco declared the Djemaa el-Fna a 'Masterpiece of World Heritage' in 2001.

An Endangered Ancient Craft

Today, though, there are fewer and fewer storytellers. In the 20th century the advent of the radio, television and finally the internet has eroded their once-important role. Where once the magical stories of the greater world were brought to life by the storyteller's tales, now news and entertainment arrives on a small screen.

Djemaa el-Fna remains one of the few places left in Morocco where storytelling carries on in some degree, but the old traditional storytellers, who spent years learning their craft through digesting ancient tales, are all nearing retirement or are already retired. For a long time it looked like there would be no new storytellers to take their place.

A New Generation

Recently there has been a resurgent interest in saving *hikayat* from extinction. A project at Cafe Clock (p94) has partnered a famed Djemaa storyteller with a group of young local apprentices who perform the tales he spins in English, bringing the rich art of Moroccan storytelling to a wider audience. Musée Boucharouite (p71) is planning to host storytelling afternoons as part of a program of cultural events. There is a future for Marrakesh's famed storytellers after all.

coffee; tea for two with sweets runs to Dh50. (☎0524 44 30 33; 32 Rue Bab Agnaou; ◷9am-9pm; ❄)

Roti d'Or INTERNATIONAL $

 6 Map p28, E2

Squeeze into this dinky place to sink your teeth into Middle Eastern *shwarma* and felafel sandwiches or hearty macaroni cheese. Check out the funky 3D pictures gracing the cobalt blue walls while you munch. (Kennaria Dabbachi; meals Dh25-35; ◷10.30am-9pm)

El Bahja MOROCCAN $

 7 Map p28, C4

Serving up filling portions of *kefta* (meatballs) and Moroccan staples to a

 Local Life
Souq Ablueh

Just off the Djemaa el-Fna is every olive-lover's nirvana – a small souq entirely devoted to olive stalls. Souq Ablueh is a foodie fiesta with pyramids of shiny green, purple and black olives. Vendors also sell olives pre-mixed with spicy harissa sauce. Buy a tub and munch away.

steady stream of hungry local workers and travellers, El Bahja is a stalwart of the Djemaa el-Fna scene. The food here isn't going to knock your socks off but it's always dependable, good value and fresh. (☎0524 44 13 51; 24 Rue Bani Marine; meals Dh60-70; ◷noon-11pm)

TIM GERARD BARKER/GETTY IMAGES ©

A Gnaoua troupe performs in Djemaa el-Fna

Local Life
Djemaa Local Bites

Several stalls on and around Djemaa el-Fna serve up the Marrakesh speciality of *tanjia*. This 'bachelor's stew' is a mix of slow-cooked lamb and preserved lemons, cooked in a paper-sealed claypot. **Haj Mustapha** (Souq Ablueh, east side; tanjia with bread & olives Dh35-50; ⊙6-10pm) offers clean seating inside a well-scuffed stall. Use bread to scoop up *tanjia*, and chase with olives.

Just off the square, **Oscar Progrès** (20 Rue Bani Marine; mains Dh30-40; ⊙noon-11pm) serves up couscous and sizzling *brochettes* (kebabs) to hungry office workers at long communal tables. Despite the dining-hall atmosphere the food is a good standard and the service efficient and pleasant.

Café Toubkal   MOROCCAN $

8 Map p28, D3

One of the more dependable restaurants right on the Djemaa, Café Toubkal dishes up a decent range of grills and tajines. Nip in for a pot of tea or grab one of its good-value breakfasts. (☎0524 44 22 66; Djemaa el-Fna; mains Dh40-50; ⊙9am-midnight)

Marrakech Henna Art Cafe   CAFE $$

9 Map p28, D4

This charming cafe and art space is a cosy retreat dishing up a mixed menu of Moroccan and international with a decent range for vegetarian and vegan travellers. True to its name there are local art exhibits, a collection of Berber artefacts, wall murals and the opportunity to get your own piece of henna body art. (☎0524 38 14 10; www.marrakechhennaartcafe.com; 35 Derb Siquya; mains Dh40-90; ⊙10am-9pm)

Earth Café   VEGETARIAN $$

10 Map p28, E4

Now for something completely different. The Earth Café, with its sunshine yellow courtyard right in the heart of the souqs, is small, but its vegie culinary ambitions are great. The warm beet salad with goat cheese may make believers out of carnivores, and the freshly squeezed fruit and veg smoothies give souq-weary shoppers a much needed boost. (☎0661 28 94 02; 2 Derb Zouak; mains Dh60-85; ⊙11am-11pm; ✐)

Café Kessabine   MOROCCAN $$

11 Map p28, E1

Snuggled right in the far corner of Djemaa el-Fna, the Kessabine may not have the panoramic views across the plaza that other restaurants can claim, but it makes up for that with a chilled-out, slightly bohemian vibe, some scrumptious main dishes and friendly service. Nosh out on a menu of tajines, *pastilla* (rich savoury-sweet pie) and salads. (☎0665 29 37 96; 77 Souq Quessabine; dishes Dh35-80; ⊙9am-11pm)

Understand
Couscous: A National Dish

Berbers call it *seksu*, *New York Times* food critic Craig Claiborne called it one of the dozen best dishes in the world, and when you're in Marrakesh, you can call couscous lunch.

Since preparing and digesting a proper couscous takes a while, Moroccans usually enjoy it on Fridays, when many take a long lunch, or the entire afternoon off, after Friday prayers. Couscous isn't a simple side dish but rather the main event of a Moroccan Friday lunch; it's served with a selection of vegetables and/or meat or fish in a delicately flavoured reduction of stock and spices.

Many delicious couscous dishes come without meat, including a pumpkin couscous, which is a Marrakesh speciality. Scrupulous vegetarians, though, will want to check in advance whether that hearty stock is indeed vegetarian. Couscous dishes can be ordered à la carte at many restaurants, but it is more often seen as a centrepiece of a multicourse lunch or dinner *diffa* (feast) – and when you get a mouthful of the stuff done properly, you'll see why.

Le Tobsil
MOROCCAN $$$

12 Map p28, A2

In this intimate riad near Bab Laksour, 50 guests (max) indulge in button-popping, five-course Moroccan menus with aperitifs and wine pairings, as Gnawa musicians strum quietly in the courtyard. Don't let the belly dancers distract you from your 11 salads, *pastilla,* tajines (yes, that's plural) and couscous, capped with mint tea, fruit and Moroccan pastries. Booking required. (☏0524 44 40 52; 22 Derb Abdellah ben Hessaien; 5-course menu incl wine Dh600; ⏱7.30-11pm Wed-Mon)

Gastro MK
MEDITERRANEAN $$$

13 Map p28, B1

This place has been causing quite the stir in foodic circles since it swung open its riad doors for dinner guests. Chef Omar El Ouahssoussi blends both Moroccan and French influences to serve up a menu that's a treat for Moroccan-cuisine newbies as well as more well-travelled tongues. Seats only 20 people per night; advance booking is a must. (☏0524 37 61 73; www.maisonmk.com; 14 Derb Sebaai; 5-course tasting menu Dh650; ⏱from 7.30pm Thu-Tue)

Drinking

Bakchich
CAFE

14 Map p28, E2

This laid-back spot is a good choice for a chill out after weaving through the souqs. Grab one of the tiny tables rimming the front entrance, order a mint tea and sit back while watching the alleyway traffic pass by. There's a decent menu of tajines and sandwiches if you're feeling peckish too. (Kennaria Dabachi; ⏰9.30am-10.30pm)

Café du Grand Balcon
CAFE

15 Map p28, D3

Yes it's a total tourist trap but the roof terrace here is *the* place on the Djemaa to get a good overall view of the carnival of life below. Head straight upstairs, buy a drink (you can't enter without buying something) and get your camera ready for panoramic plaza views. (Djemaa el-Fna; mains Dh30-50; ⏰8am-11pm)

Piano Bar
BAR

16 Map p28, B2

Step from the red Berber carpet into the classiest gin joint in Marrakesh, with powerful long drinks (Dh70 to Dh90) delivered to leather club chairs as jazz classics soar to cedar ceilings. A second plush seating area behind the reflecting pool makes a serene escape for nonsmokers and jazz-avoiders, and the terrace restaurant serves a decent Indian curry quite late. (☎0524 38 88 00; www.lesjardinsdelakoutoubia.com; Les Jardins de la Koutoubia, 26 Rue el-Koutoubia; ⏰5pm-1am)

Taj'in Darna

CAFE

17 Map p28, D3

If it's time to put your feet up after entering into some Djemaa action, Taj'in Darna is a relaxed haven on the square's rim – just the ticket for a cold-drink stop or your umpteenth mint tea. If it's views you're after, head up the rickety stairs to the large, shady terrace. (☎0670 21 31 91; 50 Djemaa el-Fna; ☺9.30am-11pm)

Chez Chegrouni

MOROCCAN

18 Map p28, D2

It's all about the terrace views over the square at Chez Chegrouni. Nab a table at the front and you've scored prime

Local Life
Juicing on the Djemaa

Get your vitamin-C fix the local way by slurping down a freshly squeezed orange juice for Dh4 at one of Djemaa el-Fna's orange juice stalls. If you're worried about hygiene, vendors are happy to fill your water bottle for you instead of using the stall's glasses.

Djemaa-watching territory. There's a menu of classic tajine options (around Dh60 to Dh70) for the hungry, though it's better for just a drink as the food can be hit-and-miss. (Djemaa el-Fna; mains Dh25-70; ☺8am-11pm)

ERIAN D CRUICKSHANK/GETTY IMAGES ©

Orange-juice stand, Djemaa el-Fna

Top Tip

Souq Semmarine: To Shop or Not To Shop

The main thoroughfare into the souq district from Djemaa el-Fna is Souq Semmarine. Site of the original leather souq, it now sells a bling-fest of lamps, pashminas and other local crafts as well as leather goods. Remember, prices are high here due to the high price of real estate on the main drag and the fact that most large tour groups will pass through.

It's always better to buy products directly from dedicated souqs, especially in the case of *babouches* (leather slippers), carpets and leatherwork, which can be found in smaller *qissariat* (covered markets).

Café L'Arôme   CAFE

19 🅟 Map p28, B3

The streetside terrace at this charmingly old-fashioned cafe has got cracking views of the Koutoubia Minaret just across the road. It's a favourite hang-out for both elderly jellaba-clad gentlemen and suited businessmen catching up on a work break which, despite its prime position, gives it a properly local ambience. (Ave Mohammed V; ⏰8.30am-10pm)

Hôtel Islane   CAFE

20 🅟 Map p28, B3

This hotel has snaffled top position across the road from the Koutoubia Mosque so stop in for a coffee or pot of tea on the rooftop terrace here if you want superb views of the minaret. Service is friendly and efficient and the coffee is surprisingly decent. (📞0524 440 081; Ave Mohammed V; ⏰8am-10pm)

Le Salama   BAR, RESTAURANT

21 🅟 Map p28, E2

The food can be hit-and-miss and the evening belly-dancing show is more cringe-inducing than razzle-dazzle, but skip all that and head to the rooftop for a sunset beer or bottle of wine. Alcohol prices are reasonable (for Marrakesh) and it has a happy hour usually from about 5pm each night. (📞0524 391300; www.lesalama.com; 40 Rue des Banques; ⏰11am-midnight)

Le Marrakchi   CAFE

22 🅟 Map p28, E2

It's all about the view. Grab one of the window tables so you've got ringside seats high above the Djemaa action. This is one of the few licensed restaurants around the square and cheerful staff seem happy for punters to pop in just for a drink. Bear in mind that a cheesy belly-dancing performance may break out while you're there. (📞0524 44 33 77; Djemaa el-Fna; ⏰noon-11pm)

Shopping

Al Nour   ARTS & CRAFTS

23 🔒 Map p28, B1

A smart cooperative run by local disabled women where you can find household linens minutely embroidered along the edges. You can also get fabulous hand-stitched Marrakesh-mod tunics, dresses and shirts for men, women and kids, and there's no extra charge for alterations. Purchases pay for salaries, training programs and a childcare centre. (📞0524 39 03 23; www.alnour-textiles.com; Rue Laksour 57; ⏰9am-2pm & 3-7pm Sat-Wed; 🛜)

Funduq el Ouarzazi   ARTS & CRAFTS

24 🔒 Map p28, C1

This slightly decrepit *funduq* (caravanserai) is a dream come true for

Couscous, Morocco's national dish

Understand
Dressing to Impress in Marrakesh

A common question is: 'How should I dress as a visitor in Marrakesh?'

Women aren't expected to cover their head. Some Moroccan women do and some don't wear the hijab (headscarf). Some wear it for religious, cultural, practical or personal reasons, or alternate, wearing a head covering in the streets but taking it off at home and work. A full face-covering veil is unusual to see.

That said, your choice of attire may be perceived as a sign of respect for yourself and Moroccans alike. For both men and women, this means not wearing shorts, sleeveless tops or revealing clothing. If you do, some people will be embarrassed for you and the family that raised you, and avoid eye contact. So if you don't want to miss out on some excellent company – especially among older Moroccans – dress modestly.

Understand
Moroccan Music

All trips to Marrakesh come with their own syncopated soundtrack; from the early evening *adhan* (call to prayer) to the donkey-cart drivers' chants of '*Balak*!' – fair warning that since donkeys don't yield, you'd better – and quick! Above all, though, it is the merging of singers, cymbals, drums and fiddles ringing out across Djemaa el-Fna that provides a suitably chaotic backing track to an evening on the square.

Morocco's indigenous music traditions fall into three main categories; Gnaoua and Berber folk music are most easily found at Djemaa el-Fna.

Gnaoua
Joyously bluesy, with a rhythm you can't refuse, Gnaoua began among freed slaves as a ritual of deliverance from slavery and into God's graces. Don't be surprised if the beat sends you into a trance – that's what it's meant to do. A true Gnaoua *lila* (spiritual jam session), may last all night with musicians erupting into leaps of joy as they enter trancelike states of ecstasy.

Berber Folk
The oldest musical traditions in Morocco are Berber and there are a variety of different forms that have evolved from the various Berber tribes. On the Djemaa you'll often spot Berber folk music by the chanting formula of the song which is usually set to a simple beat.

Arab-Andalucian
Leaving aside the thorny question of where exactly it originated (you don't want to be the cause of the next centuries-long Spain–Morocco conflict, do you?), this music combines the flamenco-style strumming and heart-string-plucking drama of Spanish folk music with the finely calibrated stringed instruments, complex percussion and haunting half-tones of classical Arab music.

Modern Moroccan Music
Like the rest of the Arab world, Moroccans listen to a lot of Egyptian music but they also have their own home-grown Moroccan pop, rock and hip hop (called hibhub). Although cherry-picking influences from the international scene, many Moroccan bands and singers manage to fuse elements of Gnaoua and Berber folk into their sound to fashion a musical style that is purely Moroccan.

shoppers who enjoy poking about in pursuit of the perfect find as much as the actual buying. Several cubby-hole shops have claimed space on the upper balcony and are a clutter of traditional jewellery, Berber artifacts and dusty antiques. Accept a mint tea from the shopkeepers and hunt away. (Pl Bab Fteuh; ⏰10am-6pm)

Kif-Kif
ARTS & CRAFTS

25 🔒 Map p28, B1

A hip boutique near Bab Ksour that engages the city's most inventive artisans to come up with clever gifts: handbags woven from recycled T-shirts, rings with interchangeable felt baubles, and adorable children's nightgowns embroidered with 'good night' in Arabic. Ten percent of the price on all kids' items goes to a local nonprofit children's organisation. (📞0661 08 20 41; www.kifkifbystef.com; 8 Rue Laksour; ⏰9am-9pm)

Warda La Mouche
FASHION

26 🔒 Map p28, E3

Those after a touch of Moroccan boho-chic style should definitely have a fossick through the clothes rails here. Floaty sundresses with quirky embroidery detail, summery tops with post-hippy flair and sophisticated harem-pant styles await to be snapped up to fit in your suitcase. The kid's clothing range is pretty adorable too. (📞0524 38 90 63; 127 Kennaria Dabachi; ⏰10am-6pm)

Understand
Henna Tattoos

This natural dye – extracted from the dried leaves of the henna tree – is applied traditionally during celebrations, particularly on the Islamic festival of Eid al-Adha and before wedding ceremonies when the women gather together to adorn the bride-to-be.

Henna-tattoo artists hang out on Djemaa el-Fna. Be careful though, because some may be using 'black henna' which may contain chemicals known to cause skin allergies rather than natural henna which is a reddish brown.

If you're unsure, both Henna Cafe (p45) and Marrakech Henna Art Cafe (p32) have henna artists on hand and guarantee they use natural henna.

Ouarzazate Huiles Essentielles
BEAUTY

27 🔒 Map p28, E3

This sweet-smelling shop with its range of argan, cactus, jasmine and amber skincare oils and creams solves your gift problems for that hard-to-buy-for friend or relative in your life. The ladies working here can also demonstrate the hard work involved in making argan oil by grinding the heavy chunks of argan. (📞0524 42 73 54; 1 Kennaria Debachi; ⏰9.30am-6pm)

Explore

Mouassine & Bab Doukkala

Mouassine is a showcase of the medina's changing face. While narrow slivers of traditional souqs are still piled high with twinkling lamps and rainbow-stripes of leatherware, a fresh breed of boutiques and lounge-style cafes are also making their mark. Don't fret though, traditionalists. In Mouassine the donkey-cart action and crumbling *funduq* (caravanserai) architecture still continues to rule the roost.

DAVE STAMBOULIS/ALAMY ©

The Sights in a Day

☀ Begin a Mouassine morning contemplating the rich decoration of **Musée Douiria de Mouassine** (p47). Then move on to Rue Dar el-Bacha to discover Marrakesh's best remnants of its caravan-city heritage. **Funduq el-Amir** (p47) and **Funduq Kharbouch** (p47) are two of the most interesting *funduqs* along this stretch.

☀ Linger over lunch, or rest tired feet over a glass of tea in the serene, leafy inner courtyard at **Le Jardin** (p51). Then indulge in a spot of souvenir hunting with a wander through the souqs. Exploring the mazy lanes around here can leave you feeling a little worn and dusty, so hop along to **Le Bain Bleu** (p48) for a spot of pampering. This private hammam mixes the ancient tradition of *gommage* (scrub) with modern spa methods.

☽ Dining within the medina is all about rooftops and riads. Choose rooftop tonight and head to **Souk Kafé** (p50) for lip-smacking mezze and aromatic tajines. Finish off the evening with a drink at **Café Arabe** (p53).

For a local's day in the souqs and Bab Doukkala, see pp42–45.

🔍 Local Life

Chic Souqs (p42)

Bab Doukkala
Neighbourhood Stroll (p44)

♥ Best of Marrakesh

Food
La Maison Arabe (p51)

Henna Cafe (p45)

Spas & Hammams
Le Bain Bleu (p48)

Heritage Spa (p48)

Hammam Dar el-Bacha (p50)

Hammam Bab Doukkala (p50)

Clubs & Bars
Café Arabe (p53)

Getting There

Walk Mouassine is at the heart of the medina. The best way to reach it is to walk. From Djemaa el-Fna, head west on Souq Quessabine until you reach Pl Bab Fteuh. Turn onto Rue Mouassine and head straight up to Mouassine Mosque.

Local Life
Chic Souqs

Who said souqs could only be old-world? In Marrakesh a score of young designers and artisans are shaking things up and bringing the medina into the modern world. Age-old beauty products get a designer makeover, kaftans have a too-cool-for-school re-vamp, and leather bags are overhauled with serious wow-factor. Mouassine's souqs are the new in-vogue address in town.

....

❶ Argan-Oil Heaven
Argan is the Moroccan miracle oil that has become a beauty must-have. In **Assouss Cooperative d'Argane** (☎0524 38 01 25; 94 Rue Mouassine; ⏱9am-1pm & 3-7pm Sat-Thu, 9am-noon Fri), the swish outlet of a women's co-operative outside Essaouira, the all-women staff will ply you with free samples of *am-lou* (argan-nut butter) and explain how their gorgeous products are made.

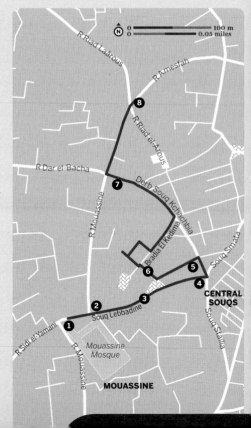

2 Marrakshi Fashion

Maktoub (📞0524 37 55 70; 128 Fontaine Mouassine; 🕐10am-7pm) is the medina's first concept store selling a range of sexy and slouchy streetwear in a multitude of colours. But where the fashion is understated, ethnic-chic accessories are big, bold and bright with jewellery from Joykech and Virginia W and super cool clutches from Maella One of a Kind.

3 Strolling Souq Lebbadine

Clustered with more traditional souq stalls swinging leather goods and lamps than you can shake a stick at, Souq Lebbadine is a chaotic and crowded affair. Look out for the sumptuously decorated mosque doorway on your right that's squeezed between two shops and check out the woodworkers skilfully crafting their wares.

4 A Soapy Nirvana

Sudsy bliss awaits a wee bit further through the souq with **L'Art du Bain Savonnerie Artisanale** (📞0668 44 59 42; Souq Lebbadine; 🕐10am-7pm Mon-Sat). These biodegradable, pure plant-oil soaps are a bath-soaker's dream. Everything is made in Marrakesh using fragrant blends of local herbs, flowers and spices, with some odder ingredients including prickly-pear-cactus extract and donkey's milk.

5 Recycling Street Cred

For something completely different, pop into teeny-tiny **Michi** (📞0661 86 44 07; 21 Souq Kchachbia; 🕐10am-7pm Mon-Thu & Sat) which fuses Japanese *wabi-sabi* (organic forms) design ideals with reclaimed materials. Store owners Hicham and Michiko have a love of quirky craft and their boutique features *babouches* (slippers) made from flour sacks and hammam tote bags created from recycled feed bags.

6 Souq Sebbaghine

Turn left into Souq Sebbaghine (Dyer's Souq) to see the rainbow wool skeins draped from the rafters. If you're lucky you might see dyers at work, but at most times there's usually plenty of colourful textiles laid out to dry and sometimes you can view the powdered pigments that the dyers use.

7 Designer Souqing

For swags of Marrakesh style check out **Souk Cherifa** (Derb Souq Kchachbia; 🕐10am-7pm), where young designers congregate in the upper balcony's salons. Pick up Berber-style beanies from Ipanema and straw bags from Original Marrakech. Afterwards head upstairs to **Terrasse des Épices** (📞0524 37 59 04; www.terrassedesepices.com; 15 Souq Cherifia; tajines Dh90-130; 🕐11am-10pm) for a reinvigorating tea.

8 Old Streets, New Fashion

Once refreshed, finish up at **MC & Joy Cabinet de Curiosités** (📞0652 78 66 91; 14 Rue Amesfah; 🕐10am-7pm) where funky jewellery sits alongside vintage kaftans and quirky objets d'art inside a treasure-trove store which puts the wacky into Moroccan fashion. It is the perfect example of how the modern is meeting the old in Marrakesh.

Local Life
Bab Doukkala Neighbourhood Stroll

If you thought the medina was all about shopping for shiny things, you thought wrong. If you've had your fill of haggling (or your suitcase is already stuffed to the brim full of new finds), head to the Bab Doukkala area to explore a quieter, more residential, part of this old city.

1 Enter through Bab Doukkala
The grand gate of Bab Doukkala is definitely looking down at heel today, but this horseshoe-arched entryway once guarded Marrakesh's northwest walls. Head through the tower arch and down the bustling local market street of **Rue Bab Doukkala** where carcasses swing from butcher's hooks, stalls display fresh fish, and fruit carts are laden with oranges.

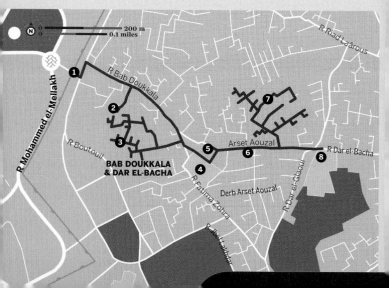

❷ Stroll Tranquil Derb Essamour

The narrow dead-end alleyway of Derb Essamour is well worth a wander for the photogenic effect of the peeling plasterwork on the walls. In particular check out the gorgeous old door of house number 11.

❸ Get Lost in Derb Dekah

Derb Dekah is a vast alley network and nearly completely residential. Here, washing hangs from iron window-grills, pot plants spruce up painted doorways and the only pedestrians you'll meet are housewives toting shopping. Don't worry if you think you're getting lost. Every turn is a dead end so all you have to do is double back.

❹ Around Bab Doukkala Mosque

The **Bab Doukkala Mosque** (Rue Fatima Zohra; ⊘closed to non-Muslims) sits beside a small square with its minaret towering above the palm trees. This local plaza is always a hive of local activity, rimmed by cubby-hole food stands with sizzling grills. It's a hang-out point for delivery-cart men catching a break in the shade.

❺ Doukkala Fountain

Swing by the furniture-maker workshops on the mosque's north side to arrive at the Doukkala Fountain. Before water was pumped into medina housing, public fountains played a major role in local lives. Although now dry, and rather decrepit, it still

bears an intricate lintel. For a close-up, squeeze past the parked cars into the fenced-off area.

❻ Henna Cafe Break

Take a break at friendly **Henna Cafe** (www.hennacafemarrakech.com; 93 Arset Aouzal; salads & snacks Dh30-80, tattoos from Dh50; ⊘11am-8pm; 🛜👣), where you can munch on a tasty *kefta* (meatball) sandwich while getting an intricate hand or foot henna decoration from its resident *nquasha* (henna artist). For a further feel-good factor, all profits here go to local residents in need.

❼ Wander through Derb el Halfaoui

Although the riad guesthouses have begun to move in, much of this maze of back lanes is quiet and residential. Derb el Halfaoui has a closed-in ambience, with plenty of dimly lit low passageways separating narrow streets, where the sky is reduced to a mere sliver of blue above.

❽ At the Pasha's Palace

End your stroll at **Dar el-Bacha Palace** (Rue Dar el-Bacha), once home of Marrakesh's feared pasha, Thami El-Glaoui, governor during Morocco's French protectorate era. Gaze up at the grand facade (the building is closed to visitors) and imagine the power this Jekyll and Hyde character wielded – hobnobbing with Churchill and Eisenhower one minute, then issuing mafia-style executions the next.

RIAD LAÂROUS

MOUASSINE

BAB DOUKKALA
& DAR EL-BACHA

R.Amesfah
9 ⊗✕11
9 ✕⊗10
R.Riad el Arous
8
Derb Souq Kchachbia
21
Bradia
El Kedima

Souq Labbadine
Musée
Douiria de Mouassine
1 ⊙

19 ⓐ
23 ⓐ
16 ⓐ
22 ⓐ
R.Mouassine

Mouassine Fountain ⊙ 4
Mouassine Mosque
Derb Tizeguarine
Funduq Kharbouch
3 ⊙
Funduq el-Amir
2 ⊙
Mouassine
15 ⓐ
24 ✕
18 ⓐ
14 ✕
Derb Chorfa el Kebir
Le Bain Bleu ⊙ 5
R.Mouassine 17 ⓐ
R Laksour
R.Sidi el-Yamani

R.Riad Laârous
Hammam de la Rose
7 ⊙
R.Dar el-Bacha

20 ⓐ

R Dar el-Glaoui
13 ✕

Arset Aouzal
Heritage Spa
6 ⊙
Derb Arset Aouzal

Bab Doukkala Mosque
R.Fatima Zohra

Derb Zaouia
R.Jbal Lakhdar
Derb Assehbe
12 ✕

R.Bab Doukkala

N
200 m
0.1 miles

For reviews see	
⊙ Sights	p47
✕⊗ Eating	p50
ⓐⓐ Drinking	p53
ⓐ Shopping	p55

Sights

Musée Douiria de Mouassine

MUSEUM

1 ⊙ Map p46, E3

House hunting in the medina, Patrick Menac'h stumbled across a historic treasure of great cultural significance. Beneath the layers of white plaster of a modest 1st-floor *douiria* (guest apartment) was a jewel of domestic Saadian architecture, circa 1560. The symphony of colours gracing the main salon's woodwork is particularly beautiful. You'll assume this is the handy work of the 24-man restoration team, but the colour and decor are, amazingly, original – their vibrancy preserved beneath those layers of plaster. For more on the *douiria*, see p52. (📞0524 38 57 21; www.douiria.com; Fontaine Mouassine, 5 Derb el Hammam; admission Dh30; ⊙10am-6pm Sat-Thu)

Funduq el-Amir

HISTORIC BUILDING

2 ⊙ Map p46, D2

This well-preserved *funduq* would have once been the staging post for medieval merchants, here to do business in the city, but today the courtyard chambers are filled with small artisan shops. It's particularly noteworthy for the red ochre geometric decoration of diamonds, hexagons and stars that border its internal stone arches. (Rue Dar el-Bacha)

Funduq Kharbouch

HISTORIC BUILDING

3 ⊙ Map p46, E2

The inner courtyard of this *funduq* may now be home to a ramshackle collection of workshops, with electricity wires strung precariously between windows, but the spacious grace and pleasing proportions of this old merchant inn haven't been lost. The upper balconies still cling on to threads of wooden ceilings now supported by plain white plaster pillars. (Rue Dar el-Bacha)

Top Tip

Keep to the Right

Sure, those zippy motorbikes and unwieldy donkey-led rubbish-collecting carts can be annoying when you're walking through the medina's skinny lanes. Remember, though, this is a living city, not a museum, and the people who live and work here need to be able to get around.

You are far less likely to find yourself dodging carts and bikes if you try to keep to the right while walking through the alleys.

And always keep alert for two-wheeled traffic sneaking up behind you. Most bicycle riders will yell 'attention!' to let you know you're in the way.

Mouassine Fountain

FOUNTAIN

4 Map p46, E3

The medina had 80 fountains at the start of the 20th century, and each neighbourhood had its own for water for cooking, public baths, orchards and gardens. The Mouassine Fountain, near Rue el-Mouassine, is a prime example, with carved wood details and continued use as a neighbourhood wool-drying area and gossip source. (Souq Lebbadine)

Le Bain Bleu

HAMMAM

5 Map p46, D4

This riad spa-hammam delivers top-notch style and value in a top-secret location. Follow signs for Dar Cherifa off Rue el-Mouassine onto Derb Chorfa, where this double riad features secluded patios, sleek subterranean steam rooms and professional services. Couples hammam/massage Dh600 per person, manicure or pedicure Dh280. (☑0524 38 38 04; www.lebainbleu.com; 32 Derb Chorfa Lakbir; massage Dh350, hammam/gommage Dh150; ⊘by appointment)

Heritage Spa

HAMMAM

6 Map p46, B2

Forget any illusions of authentically local hammams and bliss out in this private spa-hammam with a deep-cleansing sea-salt exfoliation (Dh300) or a detoxing black soap and bitter

LONELY PLANET/GETTY IMAGES ©

Carved wood detail above the Mouassine Fountain

Understand

Hammam Etiquette

Rub-a-dub-dub. Marrakesh is the perfect place to tick off the hammam experience. Whether you want to scrub away the alley dust the local way in a public hammam or reward yourself with a treat at a private spa-hammam, this city has you covered.

Public Hammams

If you're up for local interaction and a bit of an adventure, the public hammam is the way to go. You'll need a hammam kit (in a waterproof bag) of towel, flip-flops and a plastic mat (to sit on) as well as a spare pair of underwear and your shampoo and soap.

In public hammams most Moroccans bathe in their underwear. It's perfectly acceptable to wear your swimsuit – and men should definitely keep their underwear on. Take along a dry pair for afterwards.

There are three stages to a typical hammam – wash, scrub and massage. You'll be given a bucket and scoop which you fill with water from the communal bucket. Then you find a space on the floor (this is where your plastic mat comes in handy) and sluice yourself down.

Now it's time for a scrub. If you're in do-it-yourself mode, you'll have brought along an *el-kis* (coarse glove), or you can pay for a hammam attendant for *gommage* (scrub) and massage. Expect a vigorous scrub that leaves you as rosy pink as Marrakesh's walls – and half your epidermis flaked away – and a perfunctory short massage.

Some public hammams are unmarked and others simply have a picture of a man or woman stencilled on the wall outside. Ask a local for hammam recommendations. At all hammams sexes are segregated with separate bathing times for men and women.

Private Hammams

Marrakesh's private hammams are more like spas, with the most luxurious of them offering a range of add-on beauty treatments. You don't need to bring anything along; it's all provided, usually including a nifty pair of paper knickers to wear. A hammam attendant will guide you through the process, washing, scrubbing and massaging you.

Again, these hammams are segregated by sex but usually provide private sessions for couples who want to hammam together.

Local Life
Scrubbing Up Marrakshi-Style

If you want the true-blue hammam experience (rather than the one that's been polished up for the tourists), grab your hammam bag and swing on by either of these public hammams:

Hammam Dar el-Bacha (20 Rue Fatima Zohra; admission Dh10; ⊙men 7am-1pm, women 1-9pm), Marrakesh's largest traditional hammam, with star-shaped vents in the vast domed ceiling.

Hammam Bab Doukkala (Rue Bab Doukkala; admission Dh10; ⊙women noon-7pm, men from 8pm), a historic hammam, dating from the 17th century, in the southeast corner of Bab Doukkala Mosque. It has heated *tadelakt* (polished plaster) floors and a mellow atmosphere during men's hours.

orange scrub (Dh290). Afterwards, stressed travellers can soothe jet-lagged skin with a pampering massage using essential oils (from Dh400). (☑0524 38 43 33; ww.heritagespamarrakech.com; 40 Derb Arset Aouzal; treatments from Dh290; ⊙10am-8pm)

Hammam de la Rose   HAMMAM

7 Map p46, D2

This private hammam gets the thumbs up for its super-professional staff and squeaky-clean premises. There's a range of beauty treatments

you can add on, from rose facial masks to clay cleansing and a host of massage options. (☑0524 44 47 69; www.hammamdelarose.com; 130 Rue Dar el-Bacha; scrub & soak from Dh250, massage from Dh250; ⊙10am-8pm)

Eating

Souk Kafé   MOROCCAN $

8 Map p46, E2

Pull up a hand-hewn stool under terrace sun umbrellas and stay awhile: this is authentic local food worth savouring. The Moroccan *mezze* of six cooked vegetable dishes qualifies as lunch for two, and the vegetarian Berber couscous is surprisingly hearty – but wait until you get a whiff of the aromatic Marrakshi *tanjia,* beef that flakes apart after slow cooking. (☑0662 61 02 29; 11 Derb Souk Jedid, near Rue Riad El-Arous; mains Dh65-80; ⊙9am-9pm; ✻🛜)

Café Atay   CAFE $

9 Map p46, E1

There's a striking Mediterranean-island vibe going on at this cutesy cafe's rooftop, which is all rattan shades and white cane furniture with only the subtlest touches of the typical Marrakesh aesthetic on show. It's a very cool place to hang out, idle over a pot of tea, or fill up on a menu that wanders from tajines to ravioli. (☑0661 34 42 46; 62 Rue Amesfah; mains Dh40-75; ⊙11am-10pm; 🛜)

Le Jardin
FUSION $$

10 Map p46, E2

The latest idea from inspired entrepreneur Kamal Laftimi, who has transformed this 17th-century riad in the heart of the medina into a tranquil oasis. Sit beneath a canopy of banana trees, serenaded by songbirds as tiny tortoises inch across the floor tiles. Come for espresso in the morning, burgers at lunch, tea in the afternoon and tajines at dinner. (📞0524 37 82 95; www.lejardin.ma; 32 Rue El Jeld; meals Dh80-180; 📶)

Kui-Zin
MEDITERRANEAN $$

11 Map p46, E1

Kui-Zin combines top-quality cuisine with attractive surroundings. As you're munching on complimentary olives and fresh-baked bread, choose from Moroccan favourites such as lamb tajine with apricots and almonds or international fare such as chicken and mango salad, vegetable lasagne and even lemon meringue pie. Chef Kenza takes real pride in the preparation while Hassan serves everything with a heartfelt smile. (www.kui-zin.com; 12 Rue Amesfah; meals Dh80-120; ⏰11am-10pm Tue-Sun; 📶)

La Maison Arabe
MOROCCAN $$$

12 Map p46, A3

La Maison Arabe was serving Moroccan fine dining decades before other riads, and vive la différence! Here the focus is on the food and company, get-cosy booth seating, excellent classical Andalucian musicians instead of cheesy belly dancers, and the humble Marrakshi *tanjia* elevated to a main attraction. Even the scaled-down Dh330 menu qualifies as a feast. (📞0524 38 70 10; www.lamaisonarabe.com; 1 Derb Assehbi; menus from Dh330; ⏰7.30pm-midnight; 📶🖊)

Dar Moha
MOROCCAN, FUSION $$$

13 Map p46, C2

Mohamed Fedal is Morocco's foremost celebrity chef, giving tastebuds a tweak with updated Moroccan

Top Tip

Vegetarians: Your Moroccan Menu

Breakfast Load up on pastries, pancakes, fresh fruit and fresh-squeezed juice. Fresh goat's cheese and olives from the souq are solid savoury choices with fresh baked *khoobz* (wood-fired pita bread).

Lunch Dive into *mezze* (salad selection) at restaurants, which range from delicate cucumbers in orange-blossom water to substantial her-bed beets laced with kaffir lime.

Dinner Look on menus for Berber Tajine, which is vegetarian, or a veg-etarian couscous. *Briouats* (cigar-shaped pastries stuffed with goats cheese or egg and herbs) make a great starter.

The Saadians lavished mighty building projects on Marrakesh, transforming the city into their imperial capital. All the surviving architecture of their reign – the mosques at Mouassine, Bab Doukkala, Ben-Youssef and Sidi Bel-Abbes – are grand in scale, which makes Mouassine's bijou *douiria* (guesthouse) a significantly rare architectural example from this period. The *douiria* was no grandiose imperial project. It was created by a *chorfa* (noble) family after the Saadians relocated the Mouassine Jews to the Mellah and gave the city a new dynamic.

The *douiria* (p47) in its restored form allows us to imagine the lifestyle of a noble family during the Saadian reign and is an important commentary on the courtly art of hospitality during this era. Throughout the rooms, a sequence of fascinating photographs details each step of the restoration journey, which is momentous enough to appear as part of the curriculum of the École d'Architecture de Marrakech, introducing students to the concept of patrimony.

classics: quail in a flaky *warqa* pastry nest, foie gras and argan-oil couscous, melon 'couscous' with thyme honey. Lunch by the pool is a worthy feast, with orange-flower-scented cucumbers and spice-rubbed grilled lamb chops (wine is additional). (☏0524 38 64 00; www.darmoha.ma; 81 Rue Dar el-Bacha; set-menu lunch Dh255, dinner Dh530; ⊙noon-4pm & 7.30-10pm)

Villa Flore　　MEDITERRANEAN $$$

 14　Map p46, D3

Dine in this art deco black-and-white riad on reinvented Moroccan salads and aromatic, meltingly tender lamb and duck, all presented with flair by stylishly suited waiters. Pull up a sofa near the French doors or sit in the sunny courtyard and unwind with a glass of wine, right in the heart of the souqs. (☏0524 39 17 00; www.villa-flore. com; 4 Derb Azzouz; set menu from Dh220; ⊙12.30-3pm & 7.30-11pm Wed-Mon)

La Table du Palais　　MEDITERRANEAN $$$

15　Map p46, D3

Nothing beats a palm-shaded lunch after a hectic morning haggling in the souqs and this tranquil courtyard restaurant delivers on peaceful ambience. The menus cherry-pick French and Moroccan influences with ease, creating a Mediterranean fusion. If you come for dinner (set menu Dh450, booking recommended), pop into the jazzy little bar for a nightcap before you leave. (☏0524 38 50 55; www.palais-lamrani.com; Riad Palais Lamrani, 63 Rue Sidi el-Yamani; set menus from Dh170; ⊙noon-2.30pm & 7-10.30pm Mon-Sat; 🛜)

Drinking

Café Arabe   BAR

16 Map p46, E2

Gloat over souq purchases with cocktails on the roof or alongside the Zen-*zellij* (ceramic tile mosaic) courtyard fountain. Wine prices here are reasonable for such a stylish place, and you can order half bottles of better Moroccan wines such as the peppery red Siroua S. The food is bland but the company isn't – artists and designers flock here. (☎0524 42 97 28; www.cafearabe.com; 184 Rue Mouassine; ⏰10am-midnight; 🛜)

Kafé Fnaque Berbère   CAFE

17 Map p46, E4

If we're not strolling Djemma el-Fna at sunset, we're here, admiring the sky turn red over the medina rooftops on the dinkiest terrace in Marrakesh. There's a good selection of teas, the coffee is strong and there's a small menu for when you get peckish. It's just above a teeny bookshop with some good coffee-table books on Marrakesh. (☎0649 58 31 65; Rue Laksour; ⏰10am-9pm; 🛜)

Entrance to Café Arabe

Understand
Marrakesh's Funduqs

Funduqs (caravanserais) once dotted the important stopover towns on Morocco's caravan routes. Since medieval times, these creative courtyard complexes provided ground-floor stables and workshops downstairs, and rented rooms for desert traders and travelling merchants upstairs – and from this flux of artisans and adventurers emerged the inventive culture of modern-day Marrakesh. As trading communities became more stable and affluent, though, most *funduqs* were gradually replaced with private homes and storehouses.

Only 140 *funduqs* remain in the medina, many of them now converted into artisan complexes, and although you'll find them in various states of disrepair, many retain fine original woodcarving, romantic balconies and even some stucco work. The best to poke your head into to admire their well-travelled, shop-worn glory are found on Rue Dar el-Bacha and Rue Mouassine.

 Top Tip

Moroccan Tea Like a Pro
Few travellers return from Marrakesh not having supped their weight of Moroccan mint tea *(thé b'nana)*. Use the following guidelines to drink it the proper Moroccan way:

▶ Mint tea is served from a teapot called a *barrahd* and drunk out of small glasses rather than cups.

▶ Pour the first glass back into the teapot to help cool it and dissolve the sugar.

▶ When pouring, pour the tea from as high above the glass as you can without splashing.

▶ Raise your glass and say *b'saha* (here's to your health).

Dar Cherifa   CAFE

18   Map p46, D4

A serene late-15th-century Saadian riad near Rue el-Mouassine, where tea and saffron coffee are served with contemporary art and literature downstairs or terrace views upstairs. (📞0524 42 64 63; 8 Derb Chorfa Lakbir; tea & coffee Dh20-25; ⏱noon-7pm; 🛜)

Ice T   JUICE BAR

19   Map p46, E2

Every cafe worth its lemons in Marrakesh has a fine array of juices, but this is the medina's first dedicated juice bar. Try the zingy mandarin and cinnamon, or the refreshing orange, ginger and mint. Everything's freshly whizzed up in the tiny store while you

A man pouring tea at Dar Cherifa

perch on a bar stool outside on the cobblestones. (Rue Mouassine; juice Dh20; ⊙10am-6pm)

Bazaar Cafe CAFE

20 🍸 Map p46, C4

Head straight up to the rooftop with its sweeping views out to the Atlas Mountains, and relax with a bottle of wine, or beer, and some tapas-style snacks. This intimate cafe-restaurant has a relaxing ambience – just the ticket for taking a break and perusing its decent wine list after sightseeing. (📞0524 38 72 83; 24 Rue Sidi el-Yamani; ⊙11am-10pm)

Shopping

Pop-up Shop FASHION

Located in Le Jardin (see **10** ❌Map p46, E2) Norya Nemiche's Pop-up Shop counts Erykah Badu and Maggie Gyllenhaal among its fans thanks to her contemporary take on traditional caftans and *abayas* (women's garment) in fabulous silk prints. Velvety-soft suede and leather bags, kitsch clutches and a select range of jewellery and perfume from Héritage Berbère mean you can buy your complete Marrakesh wardrobe here. (www.norya-ayron.com; Le Jardin, 32 Rue El Jeld; ⊙11.30am-5pm & 7-10pm Wed-Mon, 11.30am-4pm Tue)

Top Tip

Cooperative Artisanale des Femmes de Marrakesh
ARTS & CRAFTS

21 🔒 Map p46, E3

A showcase for Marrakesh's women *mâalems* (master artisans), the cooperative is eye-opening and a total bargain. Original, handcrafted designs include handbags made from water bottle caps wrapped in wool, hand-knitted *kissa* (hammam gloves), and black-and-white caftans edged with red silk embroidery; ask cooperative director Souad Boudeiry about getting tunics and dresses tailor-made. (📞0524 37 83 08; 67 Souq Kchachbia; ⏰10am-1pm & 3.30-7pm Sat-Thu)

Al Kawtar
ARTS & CRAFTS

22 🔒 Map p46, E3

This extremely worthwhile non-profit female collective not only trains disabled women in embroidery craft but also sells some mighty fine homewares with a sharp eye for converting traditional needlework into snazzily

LONELY PLANET/GETTY IMAGES ©

Musicians perform at Dar Moha (p51)

modern pieces. Pick up a beautiful tablecloth or some gorgeous bed linen here and you know your money's going to a good cause. (☎0524 38 56 95; www.alkawtar.org; 3 Derb Zaouia Laftihia, Rue Mouassine; ☺9.30am-2pm & 3-6.30pm)

Galerie Le Coeur Blanc   ART
23 🔒 Map p46, E2

Local artist Khantour Hamid displays and sells his work in the charmingly decrepit Funduq Sarsar. His vibrant oil on canvas abstract scenes are full of the colour and mayhem of the city. (☎0667 96 75 97; 194 Rue Mouassine; ☺10am-6pm)

Maison du Caftan   CLOTHING
24 🔒 Map p46, D3

High-class and high-quality kaftans are the name of the game here, with suitably high price tags. Next door, there are gorgeous traditional textiles (bedspreads, tablecloths etc) featuring delicate embroidery. Worthy of a look even if just to browse the range of different designs. (☎0524 44 10 51; 65 Rue Sidi el-Yamani)

Explore

Central Souqs

The lanes that spool north from Djemaa el-Fna sum up this old caravan city's charm. Scents of cumin and grilled meat intermingle in alleyways where shafts of sunlight strike through palm-frond roofing and hawkers bid you hello in 10 languages. Throw away your map and go get lost in the helter-skelter for a while.

OLIVER CLEING/GETTY IMAGES ©

The Sights in a Day

☼ The best time to stroll around the central souqs is before 11am when traffic (both human and two-wheeled) is at its lowest. Take a coffee break at **Café des Épices** (p74), then head to **Musée Boucharouite** (p71) to get the low-down on one of Morocco's lesser-known crafts.

☼ Spend the afternoon in the medina to check out a couple of Marrakesh's key sights. At **Maison de la Photographie** (p64), you can see the city through the eyes of the first photographers who ventured here, then go local for lunch with couscous at **Naima** (p75). Later, pay a visit to **Musée de Marrakech** (p62) to gawp at the splendour the ruling class swaddled themselves in, then gaze in awe at the majesty of the **Ali ben Youssef Medersa** (p60).

☾ For a relaxed rooftop dinner and drink head to **Nomad** (p75) as the sun sets for chill-out time after a day within the medina hubbub.

For a local's day around the souqs and Bab Debbagh, see p66–9.

👁 Top Sights

Ali ben Youssef Medersa (p60)

Musée de Marrakech (p62)

Maison de la Photographie (p64)

🔍 Local Life

Discovering the Heart of the Souqs (p66)

Exploring Around Bab Debagh (p68)

♥ Best of Marrakesh

Food
Naima (p75)

Arts & Crafts
Souq Haddadine (p67)

Berber Culture
Musée Boucharouite (p71)

Getting There

Walk This quarter is situated at the core of the medina. The simplest route from Djemaa el-Fna is to take Rue Semmarine (off Souq Quessabine) all the way up to Pl Rahba Kedima.

If you're coming from Mouassine, rather than losing yourself within the souqs, take the longer, but more straightforward, approach via Rue Mouassine and Rue Amesfah.

Top Sights
Ali ben Youssef Medersa

Although founded in the 14th century under the Merenids, it was the Saadians – never one to turn down a grand building project – who bequeathed this *medersa* (theological college) with its dazzling decoration. Once the largest Quranic learning centre in North Africa, the *medersa* gradually lost its powerful position in the 19th century but it remains today among the region's most splendid examples of Islamic art. Its students may have long since dispersed but the building's magnificent, studious calm remains.

Map p70, B2

0524 44 18 93

Pl ben Youssef

adult/child Dh50/30, with Musée de Marrakech Dh60

9am-7pm, to 6pm winter

Courtyard at Ali ben Youssef Medersa

Don't Miss

Grand Entrance

'You who enter my door, may your highest hopes be exceeded' reads the inscription over the entry-way to the Ali ben Youssef Medersa, and after six centuries, the blessing still works its charms on visitors. Carved cedar cupolas and *mashrabiyya* (wooden-lattice screen) balconies lead the way in allowing a taste of the artisan work within.

Courtyard Opulence

The *medersa* is a mind-boggling profusion of Hispano-Moresque ornament. The courtyard, bordered by arcades on its north and south sides, is a cornucopia of five-colour *zellij* (ceramic tile mosaic) walls, stucco archways and cedar lintels with weather-worn carved vines. This would have been the main space where students at the *medersa* spent most of their day learning.

Stark Dormitories

While the students' learning space may have been sumptuously inspiring, their living quarters sure weren't. Climb up the stairs to the dormitory quarter with its series of pokey rooms with views down upon the courtyard below. Now imagine the fact that 900 students once lived here while they were studying religious and legal texts at the *medersa*.

The Beauty of the Mihrab

At the far end of the courtyard is the hall containing the mihrab (niche facing Mecca) made from prized, milky white Italian Carrara marble. The decoration on the surrounding walls is remarkably well preserved, utilising typical palm and pine-cone motifs throughout.

☑ Top Tips

▶ It's better value to buy the double ticket which covers both the *medersa* and the Musée de Marrakech.

▶ For the best photography views of the entire interior compound head upstairs to the dormitories, where small windows allow great panoramas over the courtyard.

▶ Try to time your visit for late afternoon when the light is at its best and the large tour groups have mostly dispersed for the day.

✗ Take a Break

Chill out with a tea or chow down on a lunchtime tajine upon the shady rooftop of **Terrasse La Medersa** (p74). If all this sightseeing has worked up a healthy appetite, though, make a beeline to **Naima** (p75) for some serious couscous action.

Top Sights
Musée de Marrakech

If these walls could talk they sure could tell some tales. The Mnebhi Palace was once home to Mehdi Mnebhi, defence minister during Sultan Moulay Abdelaziz's troubled 1894–1908 reign. But while Minister Mnebhi was away, receiving a medal from Queen Victoria, England, France and Spain conspired to colonise North Africa and autocrat Pasha Glaoui filched these sumptuous salons. After independence the palace became a school, but a 1997 restoration swung open the doors to the masses as the Marrakech Museum.

Map p70, B2

☎0524 44 18 93

www.museede-marrakech.ma

Pl ben Youssef

admission Dh50, with Ali ben Youssef Medersa Dh60

🕒9am-6.30pm

Detail of *zellij* (ceramic tile mosaic), Musée de Marrakech

Don't Miss

Palatial Kitchens

The most sedate interiors inside the palace are found in the old kitchens area where the green tile floors and white plaster walls hold only touches of *zellij* decoration. Now home to the Moroccan Contemporary Art Exhibition, the walls are hung with works by renowned local artists such as Abderrahim Yamou, Mohamed Nabili and Kamal Lahbabi.

Inner Courtyard

Mnebhi Palace's inner courtyard (enclosed by a roof) is a riot of cedar-wood archways, stained-glass windows, intricate painted door panels and, of course, lashings of *zellij* tilework. It's all overlooked by a whopper of a brass lamp that hangs over the central fountain. The surrounding salons have exhibits on Moroccan textiles, tea traditions and ceramics.

Dazzling Ceramics

The main room off the inner courtyard is home to a fine collection of highly decorative Fez ceramics demonstrating the elaborate blue-and-white geometric designs that made these ceramics so prized. Most of the pieces date from the 19th century when Fez's artisans were still mixing local minerals to create the distinct blue shade for which their pottery became recognised.

Palace Hammam

The three domed rooms here are a typical example of traditional hammam architecture. Entered through a narrow corridor, you reach the *frigedarium* (cold room), the *tepidarium* (warm room) and then the *caldarium* (hot room). All the rooms are minimally decorated with only daubs of simple ochre red geometric designs bordering doorways and upon the ceilings.

MARTIN CHILD/ROBERT HARDING ©

☑ Top Tips

▶ The glitzy inner courtyard of the palace is a photographer's dream, but because the roof has been closed over you may need to know how to use your camera's white balance settings to achieve photos without a yellowish cast.

▶ The museum's Moroccan artworks may not be particularly well laid out or labelled, but the real reason for a visit here is the palace's interior decoration.

✕ Take a Break

You don't need to step far from the museum to take a break. The entrance courtyard has a charming cafe with plenty of shady seating where you can rest up and enjoy a mint tea. For something more local, stroll across Pl ben Youssef to tuck into meaty grills at **Chez Abdelhay** (p72).

Top Sights
Maison de la Photographie

When Parisian Patrick Menac'h and Marrakshi Hamid Mergani realised they were both collecting vintage Moroccan photography, they decided to open a gallery to show their collections in their original context, and so Maison de la Photographie was born. Together they 'repatriated' 4500 photos, 2000 glass negatives and 80 documents dating from 1870 to 1950, and select works are exhibited here. It's a fascinating display of the lifestyles and landscapes that the first intrepid photographers captured through their lenses.

👁 Map p70, D2

📞0524 38 57 21

www.maisondelaphoto-graphie.ma

46 Souq el-Fassi

adult/child Dh40/free

🕑9.30am-7pm

Moroccan photography on display, Maison de la Photographie

Don't Miss

Vintage Portraiture

Most of the ground floor is devoted to portraiture, with a mesmerising photo of Hamidou Laambre, taken by Arevalo in 1885, being the stand-out picture of the collection. The small room leading towards the staircase contains photographs of Marrakesh in the 1920s. In particular, check out the 1926 photo of the Saadian Tombs after they'd just been rediscovered.

Morocco's Photography Debut

The ground floor's back salon holds the gallery's oldest photos, showing the debut of photography in Morocco when the first Europeans arrived with cameras and began documenting life here. The exhibit includes images of Tangier taken between 1870 and 1900 as well as a collection of postcards that were reproduced from the work of these early photographers.

Landscapes & Lifestyles

On the 1st floor, the chambers surrounding the balcony host pictures displaying the lifestyles and landscapes of Morocco in the early 20th century. Don't miss the thoroughly engaging images taken by Hungarian photographer Nicolas Muller in the 1940s – or the 1920 photo of Marrakesh's ramparts, with only empty desert stretching out to the horizon outside the walls.

High Atlas Life

As you climb the stairs to the rooftop terrace, pop into the small room where Daniel Chicault's intimate photographs of High Atlas life are displayed and his High Atlas documentary is played. Filmed in 1956, the documentary is a fascinating view into rural life during that period and was the first colour documentary made in Morocco.

☑ Top Tips

▸ Your ticket can be used for more than one visit, so if you want to come back another day and have lunch, or a tea, on the terrace, don't lose your ticket.

▸ Useful information cards (in several languages) are kept in wall folders throughout the gallery, aiding understanding of the history of photography in Morocco.

▸ For a great souvenir idea, at the entry a small shop sells editioned prints from the original negatives of many of the works displayed in the gallery.

✖ Take a Break

You have ample reason to linger after you've finished viewing the exhibits. The Maison de la Photographie's panoramic rooftop terrace is perfect for a coffee or for lunch. Otherwise, step next door to **Dar Tazi** (p75) to feast on its three-course set menu.

◯ Local Life
Discovering the Heart of the Souqs

The very core of Marrakesh is a medley of buying, selling, haggling and hawking, but it's not all about carpets, pashminas and twinkly lamps – although, yes, you'll find those as well. Here you'll see metal-workers busy at their trade, apothecaries with tiny shops full of exotic herbal remedies, and Marrakshis doing their shopping at hole-in-the-wall butcher shops and vegetable carts.

❶ Spice Action at Rahba Kedima

Begin your stroll in Pl Rahba Kedima, rimmed by spice stores. You'll notice some rather weird products if you look closely. Moroccans utilise their local spice stall as a one-stop shop for natural remedies to cure sickness and ailments, and potions to eliminate mischievous *djin* (spirits) as well as to pep up their cooking.

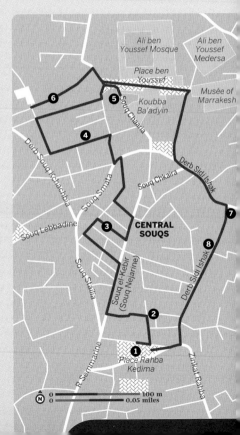

❷ The Carpet Souq

With its cheerful shopkeepers and rainbow-hued rugs swinging from every hook, it's hard to believe that Creiee Berbere was ever the scene of anything more harmful than the odd wily carpet-dealer tout. But this enclosed square once functioned as Marrakesh's main slave market where the human cargo of the caravan trade were bought and sold.

❸ Into the Qissariat

The zigzagging alleys that lie between Souq el-Kebir and Souq Smata are the **qissariat**. Although a smattering of tourist-oriented shops have moved in, they are very much a local haunt with rows of teensy jellaba and *babouches* (leather slippers) stalls. If you get a bit lost, don't worry. You'll always end up back on one of the main souq streets.

❹ Blacksmiths at Work

One of the most interesting souqs to wander is **Souq Haddadine** (Blacksmith's Souq), full of busy workshops where the sound of the metalworker's hammers provides a staccato background beat. If you've been tempted by some of those lovely Moroccan lamps for sale throughout the souqs, buying direct here will probably get you the best price.

❺ A Local Lunch

Feeling adventurous? Just behind Souq Haddadine's tangle of lanes the blacksmith clanging subsides to be replaced by the sizzle of grilled meat. The **Ben Youssef Food Stalls** (off Souq Chaaria; ⊙11.30am-3.30pm) serve up meat skewers, and the occasional stewed sheep's head, to a lunchtime crew of hungry souq-workers. Pull up a pew and eat whatever looks fresh.

❻ Leather-Hide Workshops

Take a stroll in the **leatherworker's alley** nearby where the stalls are piled high with leather hides ready to start being turned into all those handbags you see swinging throughout the main souqs. Often (mostly during morning hours) you can see freshly dyed leather hides left out to dry in the sun in Pl Ben Youssef.

❼ Central Vegetable Market

This local vegetable market is where Marrakshis living in the central medina area come wielding their baskets to stock up on fruit, herbs and fresh local produce laid out for show upon blankets on the cobblestones. For a snack, pick up some fruit here (haggling isn't necessary at the vegetable market).

❽ Through the Butcher's Alley

Locals don't need to walk far to tick off the rest of their shopping list; the lane leading south from the vegetable market is lined with small butcher's stores. Check out the entrails and offal on display, and the carcasses swinging from hooks, as you walk through on the way back to Pl Rahba Kedima.

Local Life
Exploring Around Bab Debbagh

This corner of the medina is where the workaday face of the old city comes to life. Here, the stench of the tanneries, buzzing bric-a-brac market and pilgrims paying their respects at a local *marabout* (saint) shrine reveal a city still deeply steeped in the traditions of old. Branch out from the souq's core to explore this lesser-seen side of Marrakesh.

1 At the City Gate

Bab Debbagh was built by the Almoravids as part of the city's fortifications and is now Marrakesh's most interesting surviving gate. Notice how the narrow entry passageway forms a zigzag route. This simple architectural mechanism allowed Marrakesh's troops to have the upper hand if any invading force tried to breach the city.

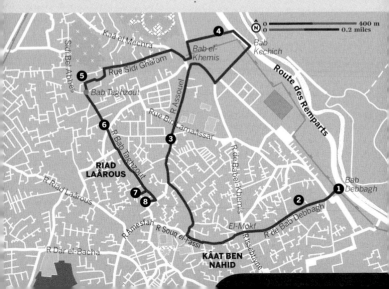

❷ Into the Tanneries

You've found Marrakesh's tanneries when you start wondering where that acrid smell is coming from. The city's tanners work through the mornings transforming leather hides into a rainbow of hues. It's hard, dirty work and dangerous too, now that natural dyes have been eschewed for chemical colours.

❸ Walking down Rue Assouel

As you stroll down busy Rue Assouel the tourist-oriented souqs seem a million miles away. No one is trying to sell you a carpet here. They're too busy doing their vegetable shopping or grabbing a quick snack from a local grill-stand while the sound of the blacksmith workshops echo over the road.

❹ Bab Kechich Market

Full of weird and wacky bric-a-brac, this market just outside the ramparts at Bab Kechich is a real-deal local scene where vendors display everything from art deco ornaments to motorbike spare parts. You never know what little gem you could unearth while sifting through the motley jumble. Stroll around the stalls until you come to Bab el-Khemis.

❺ Zawiya Sidi Bel-Abbes

Moroccans believe that just being in the vicinity of a *marabout* confers *baraka* (a state of grace) and the **Zawiya Sidi Bel-Abbes** (Rue Sidi Ghalom) is Marrakesh's most important *marabout* shrine. Non-Muslims can't enter, but walking through the arched arcade up to the gate allows a sense of the reverence still attached to this pilgrimage centre.

❻ Along Rue Bab Taghzout

The bijou pink gate of Bab Taghzout heralds your entry onto Rue Bab Taghzout, once one of the medina's major thoroughfares. Other routes have long surpassed it in importance and today it's mostly lined with workshops, tiny clothing stores displaying the latest female jellaba fashions and *passementerie* (trims) shops.

❼ Medina Lifestyles Museum

Once home to Marrakshi poet Ben Omar, the **Musée de l'Art de Vivre** (Derb Chérif; adult/child Dh40/free; ☉9am-6pm) holds a small but well-collated collection of antique kaftans and *babouches* (leather slippers) from the 19th century. There's a shady courtyard cafe where you can relax with a pot of tea too.

❽ At the 'Drink and Look'

Finish your stroll at the **Chrob ou Chouf fountain** ('Drink & Look' fountain; Rue Assouel) which still holds onto shreds of former finery with its intricately carved cedar-wood lintel. Unlike many others, this fountain is still used and you'll likely see passing pedestrians stopping for a quick drink as you admire the artistry.

A B C D

🇳 0 ___ 100 m
0 ___ 0.05 miles

R de Bab-el-Khemis

R Riad L-aârous

R Amesfah

R Souq el-Fassi

R Mouassine

Ali ben
Youssef
Mosque ⊙ 4

Dar
Bellarj

2 ⊙

13 ✕ 16 🍴 ✕ 11

**Ali ben Youssef
Medersa** ✕

5

⊙

**Maison de la
Photographie**

20 🏠

Derb Souq Kchachbia

3 ⊙ ⊙ Koubba
Ba'adiyn

⊙ **Musée de
Marrakech**

8 ✕

R Issedtine

Bradia El-kedima

Souq Chaaria

✕ 7

🍴 15

KÂAT
BEN
NAHID

Souq Smata

Derb Souq Lebbadine

🏠 23

Souq Chkaira

18 🏠

Souq el-Kebir (Souq Nejarine)

Derb Sidi Ishak

✕ 9

Souq Stailia

**CENTRAL
SOUQS**

1
⊙
**Musée
Boucharouite**

Taoulat Ben Saleh

MOUASSINE

✕ 6

Place Rahba
Kedima

🍴
17

🏠
21

12
🏠

R Laksour

10 ✕

R Semmarine

Zniqat Rahba

22 🏠

19 🏠

Derb Moulay
Abdelkader

14 🍴

R Bigui

Kennaria Dabachi

Derb Debachi

Place Bab
Fteuh

Souq Quessabine

R des
Banques

For reviews see
⊙ Top Sights   p60
⊙ Sights   p71
✕ Eating   p72
🍴 Drinking   p76
🏠 Shopping   p77

Sights

Musée Boucharouite
MUSEUM

1 Map p70, C3

Berber *boucherouites* (rag-rugs made from recycled cloth) may be a poor cousin to the famous jewel-toned Moroccan carpets, but this beautifully collated gallery housed in an 18th-century riad displays the beauty and artistry of this lesser-known craft. The museum is the work of avid collector Patrick de Maillard and, as well as *boucherouites*, the rooms are scattered with a lovely jumble of Moroccan popular art from agricultural implements to painted doors. The terrace upstairs serves refreshments. (✆0524 38 38 87; Derb El Cadi; adult/child Dh40/free; ☾9.30am-6pm Mon-Sat, closed Aug)

Dar Bellarj
GALLERY

2 Map p70, B1

Flights of fancy come with the territory at Dar Bellarj, a stork hospital (*bellarj* is Arabic for 'stork') turned into Marrakesh's premier arts centre. Each year the nonprofit Dar Bellarj Foundation adopts a program theme, ranging from film to women's textiles and storytelling. Calligraphy demonstrations, art openings, crafts exhibits and arts workshops are regular draws, and admission is usually free (there's a charge for some events). (✆0524 44 45 55; www.darbellarj.org; 9-7 Toualate Zaouiate Lahdar; admission free; ☾9.30am-12.30pm & 2-5.30pm Mon-Sat)

Koubba Ba'adiyn
HISTORIC BUILDING

3 Map p70, B2

The Almohads destroyed everything else their Almoravid predecessors built in Marrakesh, but overlooked this small, graceful 12th-century *koubba* (shrine) across from Ali ben Youssef Mosque, which was probably used for ablutions. This architectural relic reveals what Hispano-Moresque architecture owes to the Almoravids: keyhole arches, ribbed vaulting, interlaced arabesques and domed cupolas on crenellated bases. (Pl ben Youssef)

☑ Top Tip

Navigating the Souqs

Getting lost is all part of the fun. There are a couple of tricks, though, that will help you unravel the souq spaghetti-sprawl.

▶ Don't forget to look up. Many souqs have street names placed at the top of their arched entrance ways. Once you figure this out, it's easy to get your bearings.

▶ Don't automatically trust those 'To Djemaa el-Fna' signs hanging from souq ceilings. Some of them take you on ridiculously roundabout routes.

▶ If you need to ask directions, ask a shopkeeper; mischievous children (and some bored young men) deliberately mislead tourists.

Le Foundouk (p76)

Ali ben Youssef Mosque MOSQUE

4 ⊙ Map p70, B2

This mosque is affiliated with the nearby Ali ben Youssef Medersa and its minaret is the major landmark looming over Pl ben Youssef, although non-Muslims can't enter the actual building. The first mosque built here by the Almoravids was subsequently demolished by their Almohad successor, who, in turn, built their own mosque in its place.

Eating

Chez Abdelhay MOROCCAN $

5 ✕ Map p70, A2

Firing up the grill from their cubbyhole kitchen, with tables spread across the alleyway outside, these guys dish up skewers of grilled meat, with simple side dishes of lentils and salad for a tasty, filling lunch. Find it by heading up the northwest lane that leads off Pl ben Youssef. (meal Dh45; ⊙11am-3.30pm)

Understand

Medina Architecture 101

Medinas have their own distinctive urban layout and forms of architecture. The twisty labyrinth of alleyways will keep you wondering what's behind that wall or down that block. Following are some of the most common medina features you'll see:

Hammams

In past centuries hammams were the only source of hot water in the medina. Traditionally they are built of mudbrick, lined with *tadelakt* (satiny hand-polished limestone plaster that traps moisture) and capped with a dome with star-shaped vents to let steam escape.

Kasbah

This extra fortified quarter housed the ruling family and all the necessities for living in case of a siege. Marrakesh's 11th century kasbah is one of the largest remaining in Morocco and still houses a royal palace.

Ramparts

The Almoravids wrapped Marrakesh in 16km of pink pisé (mudbrick reinforced with clay and chalk), 2m thick. These dramatic and defensive walls still separate the medina from the Ville Nouvelle today.

Religious Buildings

Non-Muslims cannot enter any of the mosques in Marrakesh, but are able to admire the striking minarets from outside. Marrakesh also has seven *zawiya* (shrine to a *marabout* – saint). You'll recognise these by their green ceramic-tiled roofs.

Riads

So many riads have become hotels in recent years that the word has become a synonym for 'guesthouse' but, technically, an authentic riad has a courtyard garden divided in four parts, with a fountain in the centre.

Souqs

Souqs are the medina's market streets, criss-crossed with smaller streets lined with storerooms and cubby-hole-sized artisans' studios. Unlike souqs, these smaller streets often do not have names, and are together known as a *qissariat*. Most *qissaria* are through streets, so when (not if) you get lost in them, keep heading onward until you intersect with the next souq – or buy a carpet, whichever happens first.

Café des Épices
CAFE $

6 🍴 Map p70, B4

Watch the magic happen as you sip freshly squeezed OJ while overlooking the Rahba Kedima potion-dealers. Salads and sandwiches are fresh and made to order – try the tangy chicken spiked with herbs, nutmeg and olives. Service is surprisingly efficient, given the steep stairs. (📞0254 39 17 70; Pl Rahba Kedima; breakfast Dh25, sandwich or salad Dh25-50; ⏱8am-9pm)

Les Almoravides
MOROCCAN $

7 🍴 Map p70, B2

This small diner gets extremely popular around lunchtime and it's not hard to see why. The simple plates of panini, tajines and couscous make a filling and wholesome meal, just the ticket if you've spent the morning exploring souqs. Squeeze into one of the streetside tables and order the vegetarian couscous to get your five-plus for the day. (Souq Chaaria; mains Dh30-50; ⏱10.30am-7pm)

Terrasse La Medersa
MOROCCAN $

8 🍴 Map p70, C2

Taking over the rooftop of a small *fun-duq* (caravanserai), this kicked-back place is a fine stopover while exploring the souqs, with a menu of tajines, couscous dishes and sandwiches. It's also great for a thirst-quenching fruit cocktail. Just make sure you're not in a hurry. Service can be as chilled out (ie slow) as the ambience. (4 Rue Souq el-Fassi; dishes Dh30-70; ⏱10.30am-11pm)

Understand
Understanding Islam

Soaring minarets, shimmering mosaics, intricate calligraphy, the muezzin's call to prayer; much of what thrills visitors in Marrakesh today is inspired by a deep faith in Islam. Islam is built on five pillars: *shahada,* the affirmation of faith in God and God's word entrusted to the Prophet Mohammed; *salat* (prayer), ideally performed five times daily; *zakat* (charity), a moral obligation to give to those in need; *sawn,* the daytime fasting practised during the month of Ramadan; and *haj,* the pilgrimage to Mecca that is the culmination of lifelong faith for Muslims.

One of the biggest disappointments for non-Muslim visitors to Marrakesh who are interested in Islamic history is that they are not allowed to enter Muslim religious buildings. This decree actually dates back to the French protectorate era when French Resident-Général Lyautey banned non-Muslims from entering mosques to avoid conflict. Luckily everyone can contemplate the artistry of Islamic design within the Ali ben Youssef Medersa (p60) and also see the skilled artisan work on the Koutoubia's *minbar* (prayer pulpit) that now sits in Badi Palace (p89).

Café des Épices

Naima
MOROCCAN $$

9 Map p70, C3

If you want to eat couscous prepared by a proper Marrakshi mamma, then Naima is the place to be. Squeeze into the tiny dining room, order either tajine or couscous (there's no menu) and settle back with a mint tea as the ladies get cooking. Bring your appetite – this is family-style Moroccan food and the portions are huge. (Derb Sidi Ishak; meals Dh100; ☺10am-10pm)

Nomad
MEDITERRANEAN $$

10 Map p70, B4

Nomad takes a pared-down approach to decor with local textiles adding colourful accents to an otherwise uncluttered dining space. It's casual-chic done the right way and the small menu fuses Moroccan and Mediterranean with ease. It also gets extra brownie points for having a children's menu. Alcohol is served. (☏0524 38 16 09; www.nomadmarrakech.com; 1 Derb Arjan; mains Dh90-120; ☺10am-10pm)

Dar Tazi
MOROCCAN $$

11 Map p70, D2

We like the smiley staff and the efficient service here. The restaurant itself has plenty of old-fashioned, homey appeal and the three-course set menu, featuring fresh salads, *kefta* (meatballs) and plenty of lamb-and-prune tajine goodness, will leave you set for the night. (☏0524 37 83 82; Rue Souq el-Fazzi; set menu Dh120; ☺11.30am-10pm)

Dar TimTam
MOROCCAN $$

12 Map p70, B4

Head through the rug shop and turn right into this 18th-century riad's inner-most courtyard, where you can take your pick of cushioned nooks. Steer clear of the à la carte menu with its overpriced dishes and instead order a rejuvenating mint tea and a generous assortment of eight Moroccan salads (Dh95) for a fine light lunch to the sound of songbirds. (☏024 39 14 46; Zinkat Rahba; meals Dh95-250; ☺11.30am-4pm; ✐)

Le Foundouk
FUSION $$$

13 Map p70, C2

Like a prop from a Tim Burton movie, a spidery iron chandelier lit with candles sets the mood for offbeat à la carte choices, including beef with wild artichoke and orange-carrot soup. When the food lives up to the decor, it's fabulous, and when not, well, at least you got your money's worth for atmosphere. (☏0524 37 81 90; www.foundouk.com; 55 Souq el-Fassi; mains Dh90-160; ☺noon-midnight Tue-Sun)

Drinking

Riad Yima
TEAHOUSE

14 Map p70, B4

Acclaimed Marrakshi artist and photographer Hassan Hajjaj created this kitsch-crammed tearoom and gallery. Here all your preconceived notions of Moroccan restaurants and riads, with their *The Thousand and One Nights* fantasy of candlelit lanterns, arches and belly dancers, are revamped with a tongue-in-cheek sense of humour, accompanied with a traditional glass of mint tea, of course. (☏0524 39 19 87; www.riadyima.com; 52 Derb Aarjane, Rahba Kedima; ☺9am-6pm Mon-Sat; 📶)

Talâa Café
CAFE

15 Map p70, B2

Put your feet up for a rest on the rooftop here or perch on one of the low stools by the road to watch all the motorbike and donkey-cart action right in front of your table. The Talâa is in prime position, just off Pl ben Youssef, for a coffee, juice or tea break. (Souq Chaaria; ☺10am-9pm)

Maison de la Photographie Terrace
CAFE

16 Map p70, D2

This panoramic terrace is a wonderful place to sit back and admire the view with a fruit juice or coffee after visiting the photography gallery (p64) downstairs. It's also a decent option for lunch, serving up a fragrant chicken tajine with preserved lemon for Dh35. (☏0524 38 57 21; www.maison-delaphotographie.com; 46 Souq el-Fassi)

Chez Maazouz
CAFE

17 Map p70, B4

An easygoing place with decent coffee, great tea and fresh juices that is perfectly placed to catch the shopping-weary as they stumble out of the souqs. Head up the rickety stairs for views over Pl Rahba Kedima or throw yourself down at the shady seating out front. (☑0661 51 42 11; 192 Pl Rahba Kedima; ⊙10.30am-9pm)

Shopping

Anamil
CRAFTS

18 Map p70, C3

Step inside this little treasure trove and you're bound to fall in love with at least one beautiful thing. This extremely well-collated collection of ceramics, textiles, soft leather handbags and lamps is full of high-quality gorgeous gifts that are a little bit different, and a tad more quirky, than you'll see elsewhere in the souqs. (48 Derb Sidi Ishak; ⊙9.30am-6pm)

Understand
Carpet Buying for Beginners

This quick guide to Morocco's carpets will help you on your hunt for the perfect rug in the souqs.

Rabati Plush-pile carpets in deep jewel tones, featuring an ornate central motif balanced by fine border details. Rabati carpets are highly prized, and could run you Dh2000 per sq metre.

Chichaoua Simple and striking, with zigzags, asterisks and enigmatic symbols on a variegated red or purple background (about Dh700 to Dh1000 per sq metre).

Hanbels or kilims These are flat weaves with no pile. Some *hanbels* include Berber letters and auspicious symbols such as the evil eye, Southern Cross and Berber *fibule* (brooch) in their weave (about Dh700 to Dh900 per sq metre).

Zanafi or glaoua Kilims and shag carpeting, together at last. Opposites attract in these rugs, where sections of fluffy pile alternate with flat-woven stripes or borders. These are usually Dh1000 to Dh1750 per sq metre.

Shedwi Flat-weaves with bold patterns in black wool on off-white. For as little as Dh400 for a smaller rug, they're impressive yet inexpensive gifts.

CHRIS HELLIER/ALAMY ©

Courtyard dining, Dar TimTam (p76)

Top Tip

Know Your Saffron

Saffron – the gold dust of the foodie world – is for sale throughout Marrakesh's souqs. But hold on to your cooking aprons, gourmet travellers. Not all of it is exactly what it seems. That really cheap saffron that spice stalls are hawking for Dh10 to Dh20 per gram? That's usually safflower. Real saffron (the stigmas of the saffron crocus) have a more delicate thread, are less garishly red than safflower and have a tiny yellow tip. It costs about Dh60 per gram.

Art Ouarzazate ACCESSORIES

19 🔒 Map p70, B4

Tried and tested techniques in weaving, leatherwork and embroidery are transformed into high-fashion dandy jackets, sari-grafted coats and wire-rimmed 'papillon' dresses by dynamic duo Samad and Malek. Beyond the clothes racks there are also bags, *babouches* (leather slippers) and quirky poufs and cushions for sale. (📞0648 58 48 33; 15 Zinkat Rahba; ⊙9am-8pm)

Chabi Chic   HOMEWARES

This foodie-traveller haven, located under Nomad restaurant (see **10** ✖ Map p70, B4). Pick up beautifully packaged orange-flower water and spice-blend mixes to pep up your kitchen displays back home. Its thoroughly modern stripey tajine bowls and Moroccan tea-glass sets could put the 'wow' in your next dinner party. (✆0524 38 15 46; www.chabi-chic.com; 1 Derb Arjan; ⊙9.30am-6pm)

Bennouna Faissal Weaving   TEXTILES

20 🔒 Map p70, D2

This friendly workshop and store sells fixed-price hand-loomed cotton, wool, silk and linen textiles of exceptional quality. You're welcome to watch them work the looms as you have a relaxed browse for bed linen and scarves. Prices are higher than elsewhere but some of their products are truly beautiful and unique. (25 Souq el-Fassi; ⊙10am-5pm)

Lahandira   CARPETS

21 🔒 Map p70, B4

Piles and piles of beautiful Berber kilims and *hanbels* (woven carpets) in a range of prices. There are plenty of Berber blankets and other tribal trappings for those looking to take home something smaller as well. Get your glass of mint tea in hand and start carpet-hunting. (Funquk Namus, Derb Sidi Ishak; ⊙10am-7.30pm)

Pâtisserie Dounia   FOOD & DRINK

22 🔒 Map p70, A4

Sweet-tooth treats ahoy. The traditional Moroccan delicacies here are all about sesame, almond and sticky syrup, and make a great gift for gourmet friends back home (if you manage to resist eating them yourself). Just don't send us your dentist bill afterwards. (Souq Semmarine; ⊙10am-6.30pm)

Herboristerie Talâa   FOOD & DRINK

23 🔒 Map p70, B2

The friendly English-speaking staff here can sort you out with all your spice needs. Plus, if you want to smother yourself in the scents of the souq they have a vast selection of natural jasmine and amber perfumes and moisturising creams. (13 Souq Talâa; ⊙9.30am-6pm)

Explore

Riads Zitoun & Kasbah

Minimalism and Marrakesh high society definitely don't mix. With sumptuous palaces of long-gone pashas and sultans, and a mausoleum worth dying for, this neighbourhood puts the bling in the medina. When your neck aches from ceiling-gazing all day, seek out the *mellah;* the alleys of this old Jewish quarter are a contemplative contrast to all that razzle-dazzle.

The Sights in a Day

☀ Check out the salons of **Dar Si Said** (p86) and the exhibits of **Maison Tiskiwin** (p90) in the morning, before soaking up the quiet atmosphere of the *mellah* (Jewish quarter) in all its labyrinth lane charm. For a real peaceful interlude, stroll through the **Miaâra Jewish Cemetery** (p89). Afterwards, put your feet up at bustling Place Ferblantiers for lunch.

☀ Spend the afternoon in monument-hopping mode. First head to **Bahia Palace** (p82) for Moroccan interior overload, then say hello to the rampart storks on a stroll through once-triumphant **Badi Palace** (p89). As the afternoon light turns golden, make a beeline for the **Saadian Tombs** (p84) to see the glory of this mausoleum.

☾ For sunset views over the Kasbah area, nab a rooftop table at **Kasbah Café** (p94) for dinner. Later on, stroll to funky **Cafe Clock** (p94), which hosts a program of evening events ranging from live music to storytelling. If you fancy a nightcap to top off the day, swerve on back to Pl Ferblantiers for a cold beer at the **Kosybar** (p97).

 Top Sights

Bahia Palace (p82)

Saadian Tombs (p84)

Dar Si Said (p86)

♥ **Best of Marrakesh**

Clubs & Bars
Kosybar (p97)

Religion & Tradition
Miaâra (p89)

Koutoubia *minbar* (p89)

Berber Culture
Maison Tiskiwin (p90)

Cafe Clock (p94)

Dar Si Said (p86)

Getting There

Walk From Djemaa el-Fna it's roughly a 15-minute walk south on either Rue Riad Zitoun el-Jedid or Rue Riad Zitoun el-Kedim.

🚖 **Taxi** Ask for Palais de la Bahia. Taxis drop you in the car park 50m north of Bahia Palace.

Calèche Horse-drawn carriages, hired from their stand just off Djemaa el-Fna, provide a scenic option.

KFS/ROBERT HARDING ©

Top Sights
Bahia Palace

Imagine the splendour you'd dream up with Morocco's top artisans at your beck and call, and here you have it. La Bahia (the Beautiful) is a floor-to-ceiling extravagance, begun by Grand Vizier Si Moussa in the 1860s but embellished from 1894 to 1900 by slave-turned-vizier Abu 'Bou' Ahmed. The Bahia, though, proved too begiling. Warlord Pasha Glaoui claimed it in 1908 to entertain his European buddies and they, in turn, booted him out in 1911 to install the protectorate's Resident-General here.

Palais de la Bahia

👁 Map p88, B3

%0524 38 95 64

Rue Riad Zitoun el-Jedid

admission Dh10

🕘9am-4.30pm

Courtyard and fountain, Bahia Palace

Don't Miss

Le Petit Riad
Only a sliver of the palace's 8 hectares and 150 rooms is open to the public but you can imagine the opulent lifestyle of Bou Ahmed and his royal hangers-on within the portion on show. La Petit Riad (The Small Entry Riad), though, with its sedate blue-and-white decoration only gives a hint of the lavishness contained further in.

La Petite Cour
In the second riad area (La Petite Cour), let your eyes adjust to the dim light in the main salon, where the the palace's intricate ornamentation comes into full view. Excepting the statement fireplace, the room is starkly devoid of furnishings, making the artisan work upon ceilings and walls even more striking. Then step through an arcade of exquisitely carved arches into the verdant courtyard.

Ceiling
If you're going to envy a ceiling once in your life it will be here. *Zouak* (painted wood) embellishes all of the palace's cedar-wood ceilings. The *zouak* artists used natural pigments in their work, creating green tints from mint, yellow from saffron and red from poppy petals. Crane your neck upwards to spot the different floral motifs.

The Harem
Running off La Grande Cour (The Great Courtyard) you find the harem which once housed Bou Ahmed's four wives and 24 concubines. The quarters of his favourite, Lalla Zineb, are the most spectacular, with original woven-silk panels, stained-glass windows, intricate marquetry and ceilings painted with rose bouquets.

SEAN CAFFREY/GETTY IMAGES ©

☑ Top Tips

▶ Tour groups tend to descend between 9.30am and 12.30pm. Try to come in the afternoon to beat the crowds.

▶ Even if you avoid peak time, you may encounter a couple of tour groups. Patience is a virtue here. Come with plenty of time so you are able to admire the architecture and artisan work once they've passed by.

▶ The palm-shaded entry garden is a great place to stop for a minute and get your map bearings before heading back onto the street.

✕ Take a Break

Head straight across the street from the entry to **Café Table de Marrakech** (p97) for a juice on the rooftop. For lunch, pull up a pew at **Restaurant Place Ferblantiers No 12** (p92) for some decent tajine action.

Top Sights
Saadian Tombs

Anyone who says you can't take it with you hasn't seen the Saadian Tombs. Sultan al-Mansour spared no expense on his mausoleum, making sure the Chamber of the 12 Pillars would prolong his legend long after death. He was to be disappointed in the afterlife. A few decades after his death in 1603, Alawite Sultan Moulay Ismail walled the tombs up to keep predecessors out of sight and mind. Al-Mansour's lavishly regal mausoleum was only rediscovered by aerial photography in 1917.

Map p88, A4

Rue de la Kasbah

admission Dh10

⊘9am-4.45pm

Garden graves outside the Saadian Tombs main burial hall

Don't Miss

The Chamber of 12 Pillars

Imported Italian Carrara marble and gilded honeycomb *muqarnas* (decorative plasterwork) abound in the main chamber. All this glitz and gold surrounds the tombs of various Saadian princes and favoured members of the royal court. In particular, check out the hall's intricately carved mihrab (prayer niche), supported by a series of columns.

Al-Mansour's Final Resting Place

An opening at the hall's far end allows you a view of the central chamber which holds the tomb of the man himself. Sultan Ahmed al-Mansour ed-Dahbi's tomb lies in the middle of a dome-topped room bequeathed with *zellij* (tilework) and gilding detail. Smaller tombs (holding his sons) sit on either side of his tomb.

Lalla Messaouda's Tomb

In the courtyard an older mausoleum, carved with blessings and vigilantly guarded by stray cats, is the tomb built for al-Mansour's mother Lalla Messaouda. It actually sits over an even older mausoleum, which contained the tomb of the Saadian family founder, Mohammed esh Sheikh.

The Garden Tombs

Not an alpha prince during al-Mansour's reign? Then you were relegated to the garden plot along with his wives, royal household members and some 170 chancellors. His most trusted Jewish advisers did earn pride of place in the main burial hall, though – literally closer to the king's heart than his wives.

☑ **Top Tips**

▶ The entrance is unmarked. Walk to the southern end of the Kasbah Mosque, with the Kasbah Café directly across the road, and head down the skinny alleyway.

▶ The site is busy with tour groups from about 9.30am to 1pm and a long queue can form to view al-Mansour's chamber. Either get here right on opening time to admire the tombs in peace and quiet or try to come later in the day.

▶ The late afternoon is the best time for photography as the marble-work takes on a golden hue in the light.

✕ **Take a Break**

Conveniently just across the road from the entrance to the Saadian Tombs, **Kasbah Café** (p94) is a top spot to recharge your sightseeing batteries. Or, go local with a grill-feast at **Snack Essaid One** (p94).

HUW JONES/GETTY IMAGES ©

Top Sights
Dar Si Said

A monument to Moroccan *mâalems* (master artisans), this 19th-century medina mansion was once home to Si Said, brother to Vizier Bou Ahmed of Bahia Palace fame. You can easily see the architectural and artistic similarities between the two residences, although the Dar Si Said was built on a much smaller scale. Today the interiors of the house are a showcase of regional craft and it's also home to the Museum of Moroccan Arts.

◉ Map p88, B2

☏ 0524 38 95 64

Derb Si Said

adult/child Dh10/3

⊙ 9am-4.45pm Wed-Mon

Ornately carved archway, Dar Si Said

Don't Miss

A Rare Exhibit

Just past the entry is the museum's prize exhibit; an ablution tank crafted by Andalucian artisans, which once sat in Marrakesh's Ali ben Youssef Medersa. The marble bowl, dated from between 1002 and 1007, still holds onto some original carved floral detail around its sides and is the oldest preserved example of its type in Marrakesh.

Ground-Floor Galleries

The galleries showcase Moroccan traditional crafts. On display are antique doors carved with talismans warding off the evil eye, rare Berber embroidery and Tuareg textiles from the 18th and 19th centuries, turn-of-the-century armaments, and ceramics. The rooms lead out into an inner courtyard with a central fountain.

The Wedding Chamber

Climb the narrow staircase up to the 1st floor to visit the spectacular painted and domed wedding reception chamber, credited to artisans from Fez. Here musicians' balconies flank the vast main salon boasting exuberantly coloured cedar-wood ceilings. The rooms also contain exhibit cases displaying beautifully carved antique chests.

First-Floor Galleries

A set of stairs leads up from the wedding-reception chamber to a series of galleries. A small room (often closed) at the top is home to a collection of traditional musical instruments, while the other rooms display High Atlas carpets and textiles. A collection of 19th-century textile implements is also exhibited, including a rustic antique spindle.

☑ **Top Tips**

▶ As long as you're keeping an eye out as you walk down Rue Riad Zitoun el-Jedid you won't miss the turn-off to Dar Si Said. Take the left-hand lane (a sign is spray-painted onto the alley wall) opposite the car park and then the first left turn after that.

▶ If you ran into a tour group at Bahia Palace and are regretting not spending more time admiring the painted cedar-wood ceilings, don't fret; the upstairs rooms here are home to some excellent examples of *zouak* work.

✗ **Take a Break**

Scoot back towards Djemaa el-Fna down Rue Riad Zitoun el-Jedid for an Italian meal at **PepeNero** (p96) or have a coffee and a quick bite streetside at friendly **La Porte du Monde** (p97).

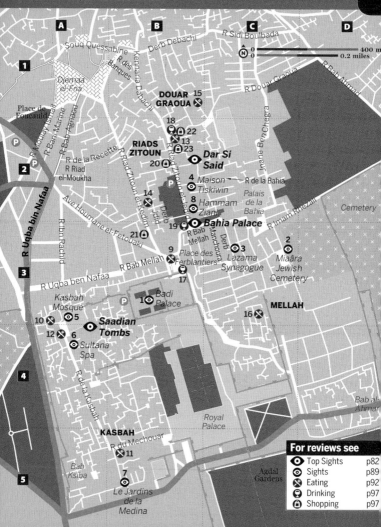

A

B

C

D

R Sidi Boulbada

Souq Quessabine

Derb Debachi

1

Djemaa
el-Fna

Kennaria Dabachi

R des
Banques

R Douar Graoua

R Bab Ahmar

Place de
Foucauld

DOUAR
GRAOUA

15

R Mouley Ismaïl

R Bab Marine

R Riad el-Moukha

R de la Recette

R Riad Zitoun el-Kedim

RIADS
ZITOUN

18

22

13

23

Dar Si
Said

2

P

P

20

Jnane Ben Chegra

4 Maison
Tiskiwin

R de la Bahia

Palais
de la
Bahia

R Uqba bin Nafaa

Ave Houmane et-Fetouaki

R Ibn Rachid

14

Derb Jdid

8 Hammam
Ziani

19

R Bab
Mellah

Bahia Palace

R Imam Rue vall

Cemetery

R Uqba ben Nafaa

21

R Bab Mellah

9

Place des
Ferblantiers

17

Derb Manchoura

3

Lazama
Synagogue

2

Miaâra
Jewish
Cemetery

3

Kasbah
Mosque

P

1

Badi
Palace

MELLAH

10

5

Saadian
Tombs

16

12

6

Sultana
Spa

4

R de la Kasbah

Royal
Palace

Bab al-
Ahmar

5

Bab
Ksiba

KASBAH

R du Mechouar

11

7

Le Jardins
de la
Medina

Agdal
Gardens

For reviews see

◉	Top Sights	p82
◉	Sights	p89
✕	Eating	p92
⊖	Drinking	p97
⊕	Shopping	p97

N 0 ___ 400 m
0 ___ 0.2 miles

Sights

Badi Palace
HISTORIC SITE

1 Map p88, B3

As 16th-century Sultan Ahmed el-Mansour was paving the Badi Palace with gold, turquoise and crystal, his court jester wisecracked, 'It'll make a beautiful ruin.' That jester was no fool: 75 years later the place was looted and today only remnants survive.

Check out the views from the pisé ramparts, and the temporary exhibits in the **Marrakesh Museum of Photography & Visual Arts** (Khaysuran Pavilion). El-Badi's other attraction is the 12th-century Koutoubia *minbar* (prayer pulpit); a masterwork by Cordoban artisans. (admission Dh10, incl Koutoubia minbar DH20; ⊙ 9am-4.45pm)

Ruins of Badi Palace

Understand
The Koutoubia Minbar

Don't scrimp on your ticket at Badi Palace: the main attraction in the ruins (if you don't count the awesome rampart views) is the Koutobia *minbar* (prayer pulpit) and it's well worth the additional Dh10 entry fee. Once the *minbar* of the Koutoubia Mosque, its cedarwood steps with gold and silver calligraphy were the work of 12th-century Cordoban artisans headed by a man named Aziz – the Metropolitan Museum of Art restoration surfaced his signature.

Miaâra Jewish Cemetery
CEMETERY

2 Map p88, C3

In this sprawling walled cemetery, the gatekeeper admits visitors who wish to pay their respects to whitewashed tombs topped with rocks for remembrance. (tip expected Dh10; ⊙ 9am-5pm Sun-Thu, 8am-1pm Fri, closed on Jewish holidays)

Lazama Synagogue
SYNAGOGUE

3 Map p88, C3

In the *mellah*, the Lazama Synagogue is still used by Marrakesh's dwindling Jewish community. An unmarked door in the alley wall (locals will point you in the right direction) leads into a pretty blue and white courtyard with the synagogue on the right-hand side. Inside the austere worship area, note the *zellij* tilework's Star of David motif. (Rue Talmud Torah; donation per person Dh20-30; ☉Sun-Thu 9am-5pm, closed on Jewish holidays)

Maison Tiskiwin   MUSEUM

4 Map p88, B2

Travel to Timbuktu and back again via Dutch anthropologist Bert Flint's art collection, displayed at Maison Tiskiwin. Each room represents a caravan stop along the Sahara-to-Marrakesh route, with indigenous crafts from Tuareg camel saddles to High Atlas carpets. The accompanying text is often more eccentric than explanatory – an example: 'By modifying his pristine nakedness Man seeks to reveal his image of himself.' – but Tiskiwin's well-travelled artefacts offer tantalising glimpses of Marrakesh's trading-post past. (☎0524 38 91 92; www.tiskiwin.com; 8 Rue de la Bahia; adult/child Dh20/10; ☉9.30am-12.30pm & 2.30-6pm)

Kasbah Mosque   MOSQUE

5 Map p88, A3

Built in 1190, the Kasbah Mosque is the main mosque for the southern end of the medina. If you were wondering what Marrakesh's famed Koutoubia Minaret would have looked like when

---

Understand
Marrakech Museum of Photography & Visual Arts

The world's largest **Museum of Photography & Visual Arts** (MMP; www.mmpva.org) is currently being built in Marrakesh. British architect David Chipperfield has been commissioned to complete the build, which is due to open near the Menara Gardens in 2016. Until then, you can visit the MMP's temporary gallery space within a section of the Badi Palace where it runs a program of revolving exhibits.

The museum is part of an ambitious plan to fashion Marrakesh into a North African cultural hub, building on the success of its Biennale and International Film Festival. When finished, the museum intends to focus on promoting Marrakesh's dynamic artistic and artisanal community through a permanent collection of lens-based contemporary art and revolving exhibitions related to architecture, design, fashion and culture with the emphasis firmly on Moroccan and North African talent.

David Knaus, the museum's director, hopes the space – with a theatre, bookshop and extensive educational facilities – will be transformative rather than static, attracting students, scholars, designers and artists from around the world.

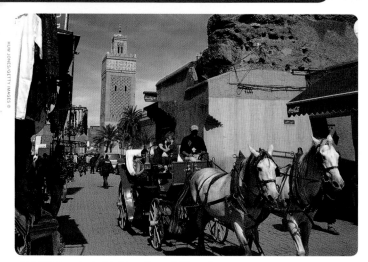

Kasbah Mosque, a focal point of the southern end of the medina

it was covered in pink plaster, then the mosque's pastel pink minaret gives you a fair idea. (Pl des Saadians; ⊘closed to non-Muslims)

Sultana Spa HAMMAM

6 ◉ Map p88, A4

An opulent, all-marble spa near the Saadian Tombs offering services from basic hammam to three-hour-plus 'absolute pleasure' treatments for couples: hammam/*gommage* (scrub), mineral-enriched tub soak, mani/pedi, sauna and jacuzzi (Dh3500). (✆0524 38 80 08; www.lasultanamarrakech.com; Rue de la Kasbah; hammam Dh200, cinnamon gommage Dh350)

Le Jardins de la Medina SWIMMING, SPA

7 ◉ Map p88, B5

This 19th-century palace-cum-boutique hotel is the most beautiful place in the medina for a light lunch and afternoon lounging poolside. The huge riad garden is planted with old palms, orange and olive trees, and jacarandas, which burst into dramatic blue bloom in early summer. (✆0524 38 18 51; http://lesjardinsdelamedina.com; Derb Chtouka 21; lunch & pool pass Dh350)

PHOTO G. MERGHETTI/ALAMY ©

Hammam Ziani

Hammam Ziani

HAMMAM

8 Map p88, B2

Not ready to launch yourself on the real-deal public hammams, but don't want the Europeanised spa treatment? Hammam Ziani is a happy compromise. There are lockers for your bags and clothes, the chill-out room for tea drinking is decked out like a highly kitsch oriental fantasy and the friendly masseurs will scrub then pummel you until you are rosy pink. (📞0662 71 55 71; www.hammamziani.ma; 14 Rue Riad Zitoun el-Jedid; scrub & massage package Dh270; ⊙8am-10pm)

Eating

Restaurant Place Ferblantiers No 12

MOROCCAN $

9 ✖ Map p88, B3

Plop down on a plastic chair in the courtyard, and have whatever's bubbling away and well caramelised on the burner. The meat and produce are fresh from the Mellah Market (p98) across the street, and the chef whips up dishes in front of you. (west entrance Pl des Ferblantiers; tajines Dh45-65; ⊙lunch)

Understand
Moroccan Menu Decoder

Let's get one thing straight. Moroccan cuisine is more than tajines and couscous, though you'll find these in abundance. Decode those sometimes rather befuddling Marrakesh menus with the list of popular dishes below.

Savoury Specialities

Beghrir Pancakes with a spongy crumpet-like texture. Usually served for breakfast.

Bessara Broad beans with cumin, paprika, olive oil and salt.

Briouat Cigar-shaped or triangular pastry stuffed with herbs and goat's cheese, meats or egg, then fried or baked.

Harira A hearty soup with a base of tomatoes, onions, saffron and coriander, often with lentils, chickpeas and/or lamb.

Kwa Grilled liver kebabs with cumin, salt and paprika.

Pastilla Savoury-sweet pie made of *warqa* (filo-like pastry) layered with pigeon or chicken cooked with caramelised onions, lemon, eggs and toasted sugared almonds, then dusted with cinnamon and powdered sugar.

Sfenj Doughnuts (sometimes with an egg deep-fried in the hole).

Tajine The famous Moroccan stew cooked in a conical earthenware pot. Classic options are *dujaj mqalli bil hamd markd wa zeetoun* (chicken with preserved lemon and olives), *kefta bil matisha wa bayd* (meatballs in a rich tomato sauce, topped with a sizzling egg), and *lehem bil berquq wa luz* (lamb with prunes and almonds served in a saffron-onion sauce).

Tanjia Crock-pot stew of seasoned lamb and preserved lemon, cooked for eight hours in the fire of a hammam.

Sweet Treats

Kaab el-ghazal Crescent-shaped 'gazelle's horns' cookie stuffed with almond paste and laced with orange-flower water.

Orange á canelle Orange slices with cinnamon and orange-flower water.

Sfaa Sweet cinnamon couscous with dried fruit and nuts, served with cream.

Local Life
Cheap Eats in the Kasbah

Rue de la Kasbah is prime territory for cheap and cheerful meals, with Marrakshis flocking to the *snaks* (kiosks) and cubby-hole restaurants for a quick lunch. Our favourite is no fuss, no frills **Snack Essaid One** (Rue de la Kasbah; meals Dh30; ⊙10am-10pm) which serves up skewered meat chargrilled to perfection.

Panna Gelato   ICE CREAM $

10 🍴 Map p88, A3

The perfect pick-me-up cure for those suffering from medina-overload. The gelato served up here, in a range of both classic and quirky flavours, would even get an Italian's stamp of approval. (www.pannagustoitaliano.com; 424 Bab Agnaou, Kasbah; 1 scoop Dh20; ⊙10.30am-11pm)

Understand
The Mellah
━━━━━━━━━

In the narrow *derbs* (alleys) of the city's historic *mellah* (Jewish quarter) are the tallest mudbrick buildings in Marrakesh. Most Jewish families moved away in the 1960s, but the *mellah* remains notable for these tall mudbrick homes along single-file streets and cross-alley gossip through wrought-iron balconies.

Cafe Clock   CAFE $$

11 🍴 Map p88, B5

Housed in an old school with sunset views over the Kasbah, Cafe Clock's signature camel burger and menu of sandwiches and salads are reason enough to drop in, but it's the cross-cultural vibe that'll keep you returning. On Sundays there are sunset concerts; and on Thursdays at 7pm Djemaa storytellers perform here (accompanied by English and French translators). (📞0655 21 01 72; www.cafeclock.com; 224 Derb Chtouka; mains Dh40-100; ⊙9am-11pm)

Kasbah Café   MOROCCAN $$

12 🍴 Map p88, A4

Say hello to your neighbours, the beak-clacking storks perched on the Saadian Tombs, and then tuck into the sizzling brochette skewers dangling on a stand. Kasbah Café wins top marks for stylish presentation of well-executed Moroccan standards, as well as Medi-Moroccan pizza and a range of fresh juices, milkshakes and non-alcoholic beer. (📞0524 38 26 25; http://kasbahcafemarrakech.com; 47 Boutouil; meals Dh100-200, pizzas Dh85; ⊙8am-10pm; ❄🔊)

Un Dejeuner á Marrakesh   MEDITERRANEAN $$

13 🍴 Map p88, B2

Come early for a piece of freshly baked quiche with asparagus or decadent *croque monsieur*, made with turkey slices and served with a tangy side salad. Ground-floor booths are comfy and quick; the tented terrace has pillows, Koutoubia views and leisurely service. (☎0524 37 83 87; 2-4 Rue Kennaria, cnr Rue Riad Zitoun el-Jedid; mains from Dh60; ⏱9am-5pm; 🖥)

Zourouni
SUSHI $$$

14 🍴 Map p88, B2

What started out as a hobby for long-time resident Yumiko – preparing traditional sushi for homesick Japanese tourists – has now become one of the hottest restaurants in town with a wait list at least two weeks long. And no wonder; housed in her beautiful riad home a maximum of 50 diners sit on purple velvet sofas waiting to be served plates of homemade *nigiri*, miso soup and two kinds of fish sushi.

Kasbah Café

Understand
Moroccan Social Graces

Many visitors are surprised at how quickly friendships can be formed in Marrakesh, and are often a little suspicious. True, carpet-dealers aren't after your friendship when they offer you mint tea, but notice how Moroccans behave with one another and you'll see that friendly overtures are more than a mere contrivance.

People you meet in passing are likely to remember you and greet you warmly the next day, and it's considered polite to stop and ask how they're doing. Greetings among friends can last 10 minutes as each person enquires after the other's happiness, well-being and family.

Moroccans are generous with their time and extend courtesies that might seem to you like impositions, from walking you to your next destination to inviting you home for lunch. To show your appreciation, stop by the next day to say hello and be sure to compliment the cook.

No alcohol is served out of respect for Yumiko's neighbours. (📞0666 74 67 28; 14 Derb Jdid, Riad Zitoun el-Kedim; 3-course menu Dh250; ⏱7-11pm Sat, Sun & Tue-Thu)

PepeNero   ITALIAN, MOROCCAN $$$

15 🍽 Map p88, B1

Never mind the exquisitely twirled cone of linguine topped by cherry tomatoes on your plate, PepeNero's interiors with its rose-filled fountains and citrus-scented courtyards almost steal the show. Housed in part of Riyad al Moussika, Thami el Glaoui's one-time pleasure palace, this Italian-Moroccan restaurant is one of the finest in the medina. (📞0524 38 90 67; www.pepenero-marrakech.com; 12 Derb Cherkaoui; meals Dh350; ⏱12.30-2:30pm & 7.30-10.30pm Tue-Sun; ❄🛜)

La Table al Badia   MOROCCAN $$$

16 🍽 Map p88, C3

This highly atmospheric riad is a top choice for Moroccan cooking with *dada* (chef) Samira at the control deck serving up her own take on the country's classics. Produce is bought from the market each day so everything's as fresh and tasty as you can get. Reservations are essential. For the best seats, reserve a table on the rooftop. (📞0524 39 01 10; www.riadalbadia.com; Riad al-Badia, Derb ahl Souss; 3-course set dinner Dh200; ⏱from 7pm)

Rooftop terrace, Kosybar

Drinking

Kosybar BAR

17 Map p88, B3

The Marrakesh-meets-Kyoto interiors are full of plush, private nooks, but keep heading upstairs to low-slung canvas sofas and Dh40 to Dh60 wine by the glass on the rooftop terrace. At the aptly named Kosybar you can enjoy drinks with a side of samba as storks give you the once-over from nearby nests; skip the cardboard-tasting sushi and stick with bar snacks. (📞 0524 38 03 24; http://kozibar.tripod.com; 47 Pl des Ferblantiers; ⏰ noon-1am)

La Porte du Monde CAFE

18 Map p88, B2

At this place, tucked into the corner of Rue Riad Zitoun el-Jedid, choose either a comfy wicker-style chair at street level or escape the souq mayhem on the terrace decorated with eclectic art and colourful wrought iron. It's a chilled-out spot to relax with a tea or coffee, and when you're peckish there's a menu of couscous, tajines and grills. (Rue Riad Zitoun el-Jedid; ⏰ 10.30am-10pm)

Café Table de Marrakech CAFE

19 Map p88, B3

Stagger up the stairs after sightseeing and plonk yourself down at one of the rooftop tables overlooking the entry to Bahia Palace to recuperate with a fruit juice or pot of tea. The food here is nothing to write home about, but it's

✓ Top Tip

Enjoying Marrakesh Street Food & Staying Healthy

Make a beeline for busy stores Marrakshis are sticklers for freshness and know which places consistently deliver.

Look over the ingredients Check the food on display, especially if ordering meat or seafood.

Clean your hands before eating Much of what we call 'food poisoning' is actually illness caused by bacteria transferred from hand to mouth while eating.

Use bread to scoop up food This is how Moroccans eat and it makes sense. Utensils are usually only briefly rinsed in cold water so not your best bet hygiene-wise.

just the ticket for a drink pit stop. (Rue Riad Zitoun el-Jedid; ⏰ 10.30am-11pm)

Shopping

Naturom BEAUTY

20 Map p88, B2

There are lots of good things about Naturom, not least its 100% organic certification and the use of pure essences and essential oils (argan, avocado, wheat germ), which ensure that all of its beauty products are completely hypo-allergenic. And with

Local Life
Market Life

For the southern side of the city, the **Mellah Market** (Ave Houmane el-Fetouaki; ⏰8am-1pm & 3-7pm) is a major source of food, spices and other household goods. Get a feel for shopping local-style by strolling the stalls. Fair warning to vegetarians: the door closest to Pl des Ferblantiers leads directly to the chicken and meat area.

Creations Pneumatiques

ARTS & CRAFTS

21 🔒 Map p88, B3

To buy crafts directly from Marrakesh's recycling artisans, head over to Riad Zitoun el-Kedim and check out lanterns, bowls and belts cleverly fashioned from tin cans and tyres. There are several to choose from, but this place (look for the framed Bob Marley poster) has a good selection of Michelin mirrors, inner-tube jewellery boxes, and man-bags with street cred. (110 Rue Riad Zitoun el-Kedim; ⏰10am-7pm)

its own medicinal and herbal garden, it has full traceability of all its raw materials. (📞0673 46 02 09; www.naturom. fr; 213 Rue Riad Zitoun el-Jedid; ⏰9.30am-8pm Sat-Thu, to noon Fri)

HUW JONES/GETTY IMAGES ©

Spices and soaps on display in the *mellah* (Jewish quarter)

Jamade

ARTS & CRAFTS

22 🔒 Map p88, B2

A standout collection of locally designed items at fixed prices. Recent scores include graphite ceramic olive-oil cruets, breezy ice blue linen tunics, citrus-seed bead necklaces with a clever antique-coin closure, and hip, hand-sewn coasters from Tigmi women's cooperative. (📞0524 42 90 42; 1 Pl Douar Graoua, cnr Rue Riad Zitoun el-Jedid; ⏲10am-noon & 3-7.30pm)

Tamaroc

ACCESSORIES

23 🔒 Map p88, B2

This tiny shop is the workshop of craftsman Adil Audalouss, who hand-stitches original handbags and satchels in colourful soft leather. If you're looking for an 'it bag' with seriously funky style, you've arrived at the right place. Adil can also create bags tailored to your own personal taste if you're looking for something completely original. (📞2638 88 69 32; 58 Riad Zitoun el-Jedid; ⏲10am-6pm)

Understand
Mellah Shopping

To see the living legacy of the *mellah*'s Jewish community, who once made up a substantial percentage of the city's artisans, metalworkers and jewellers, head to **Place des Ferblantiers** where lantern makers carry on the age-old traditions. Then stroll on to the tiny jeweller's souq, known as the **Grand Bijouterie** (Rue Bab Mellah; ⏲9am-7pm). Gold (imported from India and Bali) is sold by weight here and a few stores still specialise in making fine gold filigree work. You don't see locally made gold-filigree often elsewhere in the city as Berbers traditionally believe gold to be a source of evil.

Explore

Ville Nouvelle

Need a break from the medina hustle? Head to Marrakesh's Ville Nouvelle (new town), full of leafy parks, cafe culture, a thriving contemporary-art scene and the best bars and gourmet restaurants in town. Guéliz is the central shopping hub, while Hivernage is a high-class neighbourhood bordered by gardens and home to a few remnants of art deco architecture.

ANNE-MARIE PALMER/ALAMY ©

The Sights in a Day

☼ Catch modern Marrakesh at work by strolling through the centre of Guéliz. Sit down for a pot of tea or a coffee and soak up the old-world vibe at **Grand Café de la Poste** (p113), and then check out the interior and whatever art is on show at the exhibition space in the **Théâtre Royal** (p108).

☼ Sample a slap-up feast of home-style cooking for lunch at the **Amal Centre** (p111) before heading up to **Jardin Majorelle** (p102) to wander around Yves Saint Laurent's old stomping ground. Don't forget to visit the beautifully collated collection of the **Berber Museum** while you're here to brush up on the fascinating culture of Morocco's Amazigh peoples.

☾ Dinner decisions are tough in Guéliz. For the best of the city's Moroccan cuisine, do dinner at **Al-Fassia** (p110; don't forget to book), or if you're hankering for a cuisine change get a table at **Catanzaro** (p111) for real-deal Italian pizza. Finish off with a drink at lively **Café du Livre** (p112).

For a local's day in Guéliz, see p104.

◉ Top Sights

Jardin Majorelle (p102)

◯ Local Life

Guéliz Gallery Hop (p104)

❤ Best of Marrakesh

Food

Amal Centre (p111)

Al-Fassia (p110)

Pâtisserie al-Jawda (p117)

Catanzaro (p111)

Clubs & Bars

Café du Livre (p112)

Djellabar (p113)

Kechmara (p105)

Getting There

🚌 **Buses** 1 and 16 head to Guéliz from Pl de Foucauld.

🚕 **Taxi** Between Djemaa el-Fna and Guéliz it shouldn't cost more than Dh20.

Calèche A horse-drawn-carriage trip between Djemaa el-Fna and the Jardin Majorelle is a relaxed option.

Walk It's a 20-minute stroll from Djemaa el-Fna to Guéliz, straight up Ave Mohammed V.

Top Sights
Jardin Majorelle

Other guests bring flowers, but Yves Saint Laurent gifted the Jardin Majorelle to Marrakesh, the city that adopted him in 1964. Saint Laurent and his partner Pierre Bergé bought the electric blue villa and its garden to preserve the vision of its original owner, landscape painter Jacques Majorelle, and keep it open to the public. Thanks to Marrakshi ethnobotanist Abderrazak Benchaâbane, the Jardin Majorelle began cultivating in 1924 and is now a psychedelic desert mirage of 300 plant species from five continents.

Map p106, D2

0524 31 30 47

www.jardinmajorelle.com

cnr Aves Yacoub el-Mansour & Moulay Abdullah

garden Dh50, museum Dh25

8am-6pm, closes 5.30pm in winter

Yves Saint Laurent's Jardin Majorelle

Don't Miss

Berber Museum
Majorelle's art deco studio houses this fabulous museum, which showcases the rich panorama of Morocco's indigenous inhabitants in displays of some 600 artefacts, including wood and metal-work, textiles, and traditional costumes. Best of all is the mirrored chamber displaying a collection of chiselled, filigreed and enamelled jewels.

Garden Strolls
This has to be one of the most serene spots in the city. A circular walking path weaves between bamboo groves, palm trees and cactus gardens leading to ponds looked over by highly orna-mental pavilions. For botany fans, a series of signs along the path describe the plants in each garden.

Getting Blue With Majorelle
The blue used abundantly throughout the garden – most famously upon the studio exterior – is known as Majorelle blue and makes a zany contrast set against all that greenery. Supposedly Majorelle mixed this particular tint so that it would match the blue overalls that French workmen wear, though we've never seen workmen look quite this snazzy.

Yves Saint Laurent Mementoes
Just behind the Berber Museum is a small room displaying Yves Saint Laurent's 'Love Posters', which favoured clients of the fashion house received every New Year. At the far northeast end of the garden you find the memorial to the man himself. His ashes were scattered here in Jardin Majorelle after his death in 2008.

☑ Top Tips
▶ The afternoon is the best time for keen photographers to get the prettiest light for their snaps.

▶ Don't scrimp the extra Dh25 and miss the museum. Its exhibits are by far the best curated in Marrakesh and well worth the entry cost.

▶ The taxi drivers that hang out around Jardin Majorelle are renowned for overcharging. Walk a bit further down Ave Ya-coub el-Mansour and hail a taxi off the road – or prepare to pay way over the odds for your ride.

✗ Take a Break
Right inside the gar-dens themselves, **Café Bousafsaf** serves up crunchy salads and more substantial fare on a shady terrace surrounded by green-ery. A hop, skip and jump from the exit is **Kaowa** (p112), where you can slurp down a healthy smoothie or juice to beat the heat.

Local Life
Guéliz Gallery Hop

Marrakesh's tourist art market may still trade in an exotic mishmash of harem girls, men with muskets and other orientalist clichés, but in the Ville Nouvelle district of Guéliz an entire new generation of Marrakshi artists are spreading their wings and offering up original talent. Explore the city's contemporary-art scene to see how Marrakesh is moving with the times.

1 A Bit of Majorelle
Start off at **Matisse Art Gallery** (☎0524 44 83 26; www.matisseartgallery. com; 43 Passage Ghandouri; ⏰9.30am-noon & 3-7.30pm Mon-Sat) to check out works by Marrakshi abstract artist Aziz Abou Ali and the beautiful scenes painted by self-taught artist Ahmed Balili. It also holds a collection of vintage orientalist painters such as Jacques Majorelle (he of the garden fame).

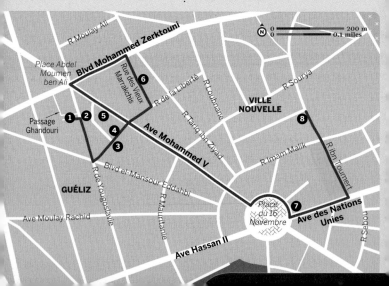

2 Move on to the Moroccan Movers & Shakers

Hop across the road to **Galerie Noir sur Blanc** (☎0524 42 24 16; www.galerienoirsur-blanc.com; 1st fl, 48 Rue Yougoslavie; ⏰3-7pm Mon, 10am-1pm & 3-7pm Tue-Sat), where a permanent exhibit of Moroccan talent is complemented by temporary exhibits focused on local artists. The well-informed staff here can provide useful insights on the local art scene.

3 Hang Out at Kechmara

Join Guéliz' hip brigade and kick back with a coffee at **Kechmara** (☎0524 42 25 32; 3 Rue de La Liberté; ⏰8am-midnight), where the daytime soundtrack is cool jazz, the coffee is strong and the walls play host to a series of changing modern-art exhibitions. For the peckish, it has a menu of steaks, burgers and salads.

4 A Spot of Funky Gift Shopping

Break up the art-viewing with a browse at the original jewellery, hip accessories and some extremely cute children's soft toys in **Côté Sud** (☎0524 43 84 48; Rue de la Liberté; ⏰9.30am-6pm). You'll find products made by some of Marrakesh's coolest artisans for sale at this dinky shop.

5 Check Out Some Snaps

Move on to **Gallery 127** (☎0524 43 26 67; www.galerienathalielocatelli.com; 2nd fl, 127 Ave Mohammed V; ⏰3-7pm Tue-Sat), found by taking a once-grand stairway up to its industrial-chic art space. It exhibits a range of new and vintage works by international photographers at reasonable prices. Afterwards, visit bustling Boulevard Mohamed Zerktouni to capture a sense of modern Marrakesh at work.

6 Dive into an Abstract World

In the **David Bloch Gallery** (☎0524 45 75 95; www.davidblochgallery.com; 8 bis Rue des Vieux Marrakchis; ⏰10.30am-1.30pm & 3.30-7.30pm Tue-Sat, 3.30-7.30pm Mon) artists from both sides of the Mediterranean strike fine lines between traditional calligraphy and urban graffiti in a series of temporary exhibitions. Here, you can catch the work of the scene's young up-and-coming abstract artists.

7 Snack at Café 16

Nab an outdoor table at **Café 16** (☎0524 33 96 70; 18 Pl du 16 Novembre; desserts Dh20-50; ⏰9am-midnight), which blends European style with a warm Marrakshi welcome. Have a light salad or sandwich snack then dig into its intriguing ice-cream flavours, such as mint tea and *kaab el-gazelle* (almond cookie) or treat yourself to its divine raspberry mousse cake.

8 View the Next Big Thing

To finish off, check out the next generation of Moroccan art stars at **Galerie Ré** (☎0524 43 22 58; www.galeriere.com; Résidence Al Andalous III, cnr Rues de la Mosquée & Ibn Toumert; ⏰10am-1pm & 3-8pm Mon-Sat). Both the permanent and temporary galleries at this supersuave space host a wealth of emerging talent from across North Africa.

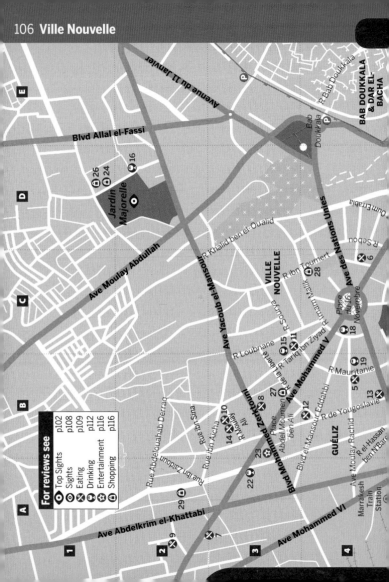

Avenue du 11 Janvier

P

R. Bab Doukkala

BAB DOUKKALA
& DAR EL-BACHA

Bab Doukkala

Blvd Allal el-Fassi

P

26
24

16

Jardin Majorelle

Oum Errabia

R Khalid ben el-Oualid

R. Sebou

Ave Moulay Abdullah

Ave Yacoub el-Mansour

VILLE NOUVELLE

R Ibn Toumert

28

Ave des Nations Unies

R Loubnane

R Tariq ibn Ziyad

R Imam Malik

15
11

Place du 16 Novembre

Rue Abdelouahab Derraq

Rue Ibn Sina

Rue Aicha

R Moulay Ali

14
10

Place Abdel Moumen ben Ali

R de Liberté

R Tariq ibn Ziyad

Ave Mohammed V

R Mauritanie

5
13

18

19

Blvd Mohammed Zerktouni

27

8

Blvd el-Mansour Eddahbi

12

R de Yougoslavie

GUÉLIZ

Ave Moulay Rachid

R el-Hassan ben N'Barc

Rue Ibn Zaidoun

23

22

29

9

Ave Abdelkrim el-Khattabi

7

Ave Mohammed VI

Marrakesh Train Station

For reviews see

⊙	Top Sights	p102
◉	Sights	p108
⊗	Eating	p109
🍷	Drinking	p112
🎭	Entertainment	p116
🛍	Shopping	p116

Ave Bab Jedid

La Mamounia Gardens

3

Bab el Jedid

CyberPark

Bab Nkob

1

Ave el-Yarmouk

R Harun Errachid

R Haroun Errachid

21

Place de la Liberté

Ave Echouhada

R Ibrahim el Mazini

20

Ave de la Menara

ve Yacoub al-Mansur

17

R Mohammed el-Hassan

HIVERNAGE

R de Paris

R Qâdi el Makhazin

R de Paris

Ave el-Qadissa

4

Jardin Harti

Ave du Président Kennedy

Ave Mohammed VI

R el-Qâdi Ayâd

Théâtre Royal

2

R Abou Bakr Seddiq

R el-Jahed

Ave Hassan II

500 m

0.25 miles

N

0

0

Sights

CyberPark
GARDENS

1 Map p106, D5

Stop and smell the roses at this 8-hectare royal garden, dating from the 18th century. It now offers free wi-fi at outdoor kiosks and an air-conditioned cybercafe (Dh10 per hour) – hence the park's less-than-regal name. This garden is a well-maintained and shady retreat, popular with young couples and early-evening strollers. (Ave Mohammed V; admission free; ⏱9am-7pm)

✅ Top Tip
Marrakesh Taxi Debacle

You may want to use a taxi when journeying between the medina and the Ville Nouvelle. All petits taxis (local taxis) are suppposed to use a meter. Unfortunately someone forgot to send the drivers this memo.

▶ To ask in French for the meter to be switched on, say '*tourne le conteur, si'l vous plait*'.

▶ If the driver refuses and is quoting a ridiculous price, ask to stop and get out.

▶ Hail off the street. Taxis milling in ranks are usually the worst offenders.

▶ Don't get upset. Marrakesh taxis are notorious for overcharging visitors. It's not worth ruining your day over.

Théâtre Royal
GALLERY

2 Map p106, B5

Begun in the 1970s by Tunisian architect Charles Boccara, this grand edifice is still yet to be completed. Today the entrance foyer, and its balconies, host temporary art exhibitions, but you're really here to see the impressive interior with its domed ceiling, brickwork detailing and woodwork flourishes that merge Moroccan and European styles. A caretaker may offer to show you the huge unfinished opera house for a small tip. The smaller, completed outdoor theatre at the back hosts major productions. (Ave Hassan II, Guéliz; admission free; ⏱9.30am-5pm)

La Mamounia Gardens
PARK

3 Map p106, E7

On their trips to Marrakesh, Winston Churchill and Franklin D Roosevelt spent their downtime here, among the rose bushes and ornamental shrubbery that belong to the luxurious La Mamounia Hotel. These days the garden isn't as elegantly kept up as it must have been in its glory days, but it's still a relaxing spot to get away from the hurly-burly of the city. Don't dress too scruffily if you want the doormen on the hotel gate to let you in. (Ave Houmane el-Fetouaki; admission free)

Jardin Harti
PARK

4 Map p106, C5

Slap in the centre of Guéliz, this tranquil park is full of palm-tree-shaded

La Mamounia Gardens

benches and flower beds that bloom through summer. The two life-sized dinosaurs make it also a favourite hang-out for local families out for a weekend stroll. (Rue Ouadi el-Makhazine; admission free; ⏰8am-6pm; 👶)

Eating

Samak al-Bahriya SEAFOOD $

 5 Map p106, B4

Fish and chips the Marrakesh way. The entire stretch of Rue Mauritanie is packed with pavement stalls and restaurants serving up seafood offerings, but Samak al-Bahriya is our favourite for dishing up fresh fish and perfectly tender fried calamari with generous chunks of lemon, plus salt, cumin and hot sauce. (75 Ave Moulay Rachid, cnr Rue Mauritanie; seafood with chips Dh30-80; ⏰10am-midnight)

Eveil des Sens INTERNATIONAL $

 6 Map p106, C4

If you're hunting for a cheap and cheerful meal in Guéliz, this super-friendly, casual restaurant hits the spot nicely. There's all the usual couscous, tajine and brochette (kebab), but also pizza and seafood dishes for the tajine-weary. No, it won't win any awards for gourmet innovation; this is just hearty portions of simple dishes served with a smile. (☏0524 45 86 17; 32 Rue Ibn Atya; mains Dh45-80; ⏰noon-11pm Tue-Sun)

Panna Gelato
ICE CREAM **$**

7 Map p106, A3

A master gelato artisan from Italy, proprietary recipes and top ingredients make Panna the best place for ice cream in Morocco. It has another branch in the medina's kasbah as well. (📞0524 43 65 65; www.pannagustoitaliano.com; cnr Rue du Capitaine Arrigui; cones Dh20; ⏱7.30am-10pm; ❄🚻)

Al-Fassia
MOROCCAN **$$**

8 Map p106, B3

The nine-dish mezze (starter-style plates) is a proper feast on its own, but there's no resisting the classic mains, such as Berber pumpkin-and-lamb tajine, perfected over a decade by the Marrakshi sisters who own the place. Reservations are essential.

(📞0524 43 40 60; http://alfassia.com; 55 Blvd Mohammed Zerktouni; meals Dh180-250; ⏱noon-2.30pm & 7.30-11pm Wed-Sun)

La Cuisine de Mona
LEBANESE **$$**

9 Map p106, A2

Tiny and tasty, Mona's serves delicious, vegetarian-friendly food on painted plates in a colourful, modern venue. If you can, grab one of the three tables outside and wait for a parade of mezze, including citrus-glazed chicken wings, classic baba ghanoush, chicken livers, hummus and fresh vegetables with a minty yoghurt dip. There are even a few bottles of Lebanese wine on the menu, or fruit cocktails for non-drinkers. (📞0618 13 79 59; http://lacuisinedemona.com; 5 Residence Mamoune, 115B; meals Dh70-120; ⏱10am-10.30pm Mon-Sat; 🖊)

Understand
The Making of Ville Nouvelle

When Morocco came under colonial control, villes nouvelles (new towns) were built outside the walls of old city medinas, with street grids and modern architecture imposing strict order. Neoclassical facades, mansard roofs and high-rises must have come as quite a shock when they were introduced by the French.

But one style that seemed to bridge local Islamic geometry and streamlined European modernism was art deco. Painter Jacques Majorelle brought a Moroccan colour sensibility to deco in 1924, adding bursts of blue, green and acid yellow to his villa and Jardin Majorelle.

In the 1930s architects began cleverly grafting Moroccan geometric detail onto whitewashed European edifices, creating a signature Moroccan art deco style that became known as Mauresque-deco. You can still see elements of this style in many of the older buildings in Marrakesh's Ville Nouvelle.

Chez Mado

SEAFOOD $$

10 Map p106, B3

With the fragrance of Oualidia's salty shallows still fresh on them, Chez Mado's oysters are the prettiest and plumpest in Marrakesh. Shellfish and seafood are delivered daily here, and under chef Alex Chaussetier's direction they are transformed into the lightest lunches: elegant sole *meunière*, grilled prawns and mayonnaise, John Dory with chorizo and a seafood platter to blow your mind. (☏0524 42 14 94; www.chezmado-marrakech.com; 22 Rue Moulay Ali; menu du jour Dh100-120, meals Dh250-350; ☺noon-3pm & 7.30-11.30pm Tue-Sun; ❄)

Catanzaro

ITALIAN $$

11 Map p106, C3

Where are we, exactly? The thin-crust, wood-fired pizza says Italy, the wooden balcony and powerful air-con suggest the Alps, but the spicy condiments and spicier clientele are definitely midtown Marrakesh. Grilled meat dishes are juicy and generous, but the Neapolitan pizza with capers, local olives and Atlantic anchovies steals the show. (☏0524 43 37 31; 42 Rue Tariq ibn Ziyad; pizzas Dh60-80, meals Dh100-150; ☺noon-2.30pm & 7.15-11pm Mon-Sat; ❄)

Mamma Mia

ITALIAN $$

12 Map p106, B4

This family-friendly Italian trattoria packs in punters with good-value

pizzas and generous bowls of pasta alongside classic Italian dishes such as *osso buco*. It also has a good selection of charcuterie (cured meats). Exposed brickwork, red-and-white-checked tablecloths and vintage 1950s posters make for a warm and laid-back atmosphere. Families should come early before the smoking crowd gets

---

Local Life

Office-Worker Lunch

On weekday lunchtimes local office workers descend in droves on the string of restaurants along **Rue ibn Aicha** in Guéliz to refuel on grilled-meat goodness, well-caramelised tajines and offal offerings. Grab a table at whichever restaurant you fancy and join in.

---

comfortable at 9pm. (☏0524 43 44 54; www.mammamia-marrakech.com; 18 Rue de la Liberté; meals Dh50-170; ☺noon-11pm; ☺)

Azar
MIDDLE EASTERN $$$

13 ☒ Map p106, B4

Imagine a Beirut lounge teleported to Marrakesh via Mars: with space-captain chairs and star-patterned stucco walls, the decor is out of this world – and the Lebanese-inspired fare isn't far behind. Authenticity sticklers will appreciate the *shish taouk* (plump marinated chicken cubes), and the shared mezze with Dh50 glasses of wine will keep vegetarians happy and bills in this stratosphere. (☏0524 43 09 20; www.azarmarrakech.com; cnr Ave Hassan II & Rue de Yougoslavie; meals Dh180-250; ☺noon-3pm & 7pm-midnight; ❄☺)

L'Annexe
FRENCH $$$

14 ☒ Map p106, B3

French lunches in a mirrored cafe-bistro setting, handy to all the Ville Nouvelle boutique action. After the umpteenth tajine, L'Annexe offers a welcome switch to light, clean flavours: Provençal fish soup, *duck confit* (duck slowly cooked in its own fat) atop salad and a mean crème brûlée. (☏0524 43 40 10; www.lannexemarrakech. com; 14 Rue Moulay Ali; meals Dh200-250; ☺noon-3.30pm & 7.30-11:30pm Mon-Sat; ☺)

Drinking

Café du Livre
CAFE

15 ☺ Map p106, C3

A bookish beauty, with walls of used books in English and French to browse, board games, decently priced draught beer, cushy seating, quiz nights and poetry readings, plus free wi-fi and tasty salads (Dh55-90). By far the Ville Nouvelle's most chilled-out cafe. After dark it takes on a pub atmosphere and the music gets pumped up. (☏0524 43 21 49; www.cafedulivre.com; 44 Rue Tariq ibn Ziyad; ☺9.30am-9pm Mon-Sat; ☺)

Kaowa
CAFE

16 ☺ Map p106, D2

Breezy Kaowa brings a touch of California cool to the Majorelle gardens with a juice bar stacked with watermelon, blood oranges, lemons and pomegranates. Drink detox smoothies on the decked terrace and, if hungry, munch on vegetarian wraps and *briouat* (filo-pastry parcels) inside. (☏0524 33 00 72; 34 Rue Yves Saint Laurent; ☺9am-6pm; ☺)

LOOK DIE BILDAGENTUR DER FOTOGRAFEN GMBH/ALAMY ©

Djellabar

Djellabar BAR

17 Map p106, C5

A fashion-forward crowd flocks to Claude Challe's newest venture for its fusion menu and playful pop-art aesthetic. Challe's Maroc n'Roll style works a treat in this converted stucco-tastic 1940s wedding hall with an eye-popping *zellij*-backed bar, snakeskin loungers and a collection of portraits of fez-wearing icons from Marilyn Monroe to Nelson Mandela. (0524 42 12 42; 2 Rue Abou Hanifa, Hivernage; cocktails Dh100; 7pm-2am)

Grand Café de la Poste CAFE

18 Map p106, C4

Restored to its flapper-era glory, this landmark bistro delivers swanky comfort and the best wine list in town. Prices run high for dinner, and service can be agonisingly slow, but during the 6pm to 8pm happy hour, a parade of appetisers is offered with drinks – so skip the meal and lap up this cafe's history, wine in hand. (0524 43 30 38; Blvd el-Mansour Eddahbi, cnr Rue Imam Malik; meals Dh180-300; 8am-1am)

Understand

Marrakesh Haggling Guide

Haggling can be great fun as long as you go into it with the right attitude. Don't try out your bargaining skills when you're tired and grumpy. You're not likely to make a great deal and it will be a thoroughly unenjoyable experience.

The most important note to remember is that both you and the seller are trying to reach an agreement that satisfies both of you. The vendor is not going to sell an object for a loss and if you can't reach a mutually beneficial price, you simply walk away.

▶ Exchange pleasantries first with the shopkeeper. Don't even think about kicking off negotiations without saying hello and asking how they are.

▶ If you see something you like, work out what you're willing to pay for it before you ask the price.

▶ The initial price the vendor quotes may have nothing to do with the item's actual value, so don't rely on that figure for your counteroffer. Depending on the vendor (and their perception of how much money you may have) their first quote may be exceedingly high or not far off the value of the item. This is why it's important that you've already worked out what your maximum offering will be.

▶ Counter with an offer about one third of your maximum limit and let the negotiations begin. Keep it friendly. Bargaining should never get nasty. If you're starting to feel pressured or you get a bad vibe from the seller, walk away.

▶ Walking away when you can't reach an agreement is fine. Offering a price you're not willing to pay and then walking away is considered the height of bad manners. Make sure you actually want the item before starting to haggle.

A Couple of Other Pointers

▶ You don't haggle for groceries. If you're buying fruit at the produce market, you're being quoted the actual price.

▶ Spend time perusing prices at fixed-price stores such as Ensemble Artisanal (p116) beforehand, to get an idea of costs.

▶ Never shop with a guide if you want the best price. The shopkeeper has to add their commission onto your bill.

Le Studio
BAR

19 Map p106, B4

This upmarket winebar-cum-restaurant serves up a sophisticated wine list and some impeccable French food. Perch at high tables, sipping smooth glasses of Domaine de Sahari and nibbling on spiced olives, or dine beneath the open, retractable roof, mopping up plates of lobster fricassee and beef fillet dusted with truffle shavings. Suave hosts Steeve and Didier circle the room lapping up compliments. (☎0524 43 37 00; 85 Ave Moulay Rachid; meal Dh200-250; 🛜)

Theatro
CLUB

20 Map p106, D7

The most convenient club in Marrakesh is the old-time favourite Theatro, actually located as its name suggests in an old theatre. Themed nights, bizarre floor shows with acrobats and jugglers and a lively mix of house, R&B and Middle Eastern pop keep the punters coming. A recent collaboration saw Wednesday nights dedicated to aspiring Marrakshi DJs, dancers and performers. (☎0524 44 88 11; www.theatromarrakech.com; Hôtel es Saadi, Rue Ibrahim el Mazini; admission Dh200; ⏱11.30pm-5am)

Churchill Bar
BAR

In Marrakesh's landmark La Mamounia Hotel (see 3 ⦿Map p106, E7), the bar named for the Mamounia regular and sometime head of state retains its

Top Tip
Fancy a Tipple?

Alcohol isn't widely served at medina restaurants, so head for the Ville Nouvelle if you want a drink. Moroccan wines are definitely worth a try. Look for these names when you're choosing your bottle:

White Try crisp, food-friendly Larroque; well-balanced, juicy Terre Blanche; and citrusy, off-dry Cuveé du Président Sémillant.

Gris & Rosé Look for not-too-fruity Medaillon Rosé de Syrah; fragrant Domaine Rimal Vin Gris; and the crisply top-range Volubilia.

Red Reliable reds include the admirable Burgundian-style Terre Rouge from Rabati coastal vineyards; well-rounded Volubilia from Morocco's ancient Roman wine-growing region; and spicier merlot-syrah-cabernet sauvignon Coteaux Atlas.

speakeasy appeal, with fuchsia leather, wood panelling and splashy leopard print. Dress to impress and go retro with a Mamoune Lady: gin, lemon and orange-flower water. At about €20 per cocktail, let heads of state buy the first round. (☎0524 38 86 00; www.mamounia.com; La Mamounia, Ave Houmane el-Fetouaki; ⏱6pm-1am; 🛜)

Top Tip
Self-Catering

Self-caterers and visitors searching for hard-to-find items in the medina such as nappies and baby food should head to Guéliz to stock up.

Carrefour (Eden Centre, Ave Mohammed V; ⊙9am-11pm) is right in the centre of Guéliz and stocks a large selection of international brands, a deli-selection full of specialities, an alcohol section and baby products.

ACIMA (Ave Yacoub el-Mansour; ⊙9am-10pm) doesn't have quite as good a variety but does stock nappies, other baby products and most essential groceries, and is handily situated by Jardin Majorelle.

Comptoir   BAR

 21 Map p106, D6

Never mind the restaurant downstairs; the flash lounge upstairs is the place for visiting fashion designers and married Casa playboys to mingle over cocktails. There's no avoiding the belly dancers, who descend en masse every other hour. (☑0524 43 77 02; www.comptoirdarna.com; Ave Echouhada; ⊙4pm-2am)

Sky Bar 23   BAR

22 Map p106, A3

The rooftop bar of the Renaissance Hotel is the best Ville Nouvelle option for a drink with a view. Canoodling couples sneak up to the shadowy corners of the top deck for great drinks and a view of city lights framing the giant, retro, red

neon 'Bar' sign that bathes the hotel terrace in a rosy glow. (www.renaissance-hotel-marrakech.com; Renaissance Hotel, Ave Mohammed V; ⊙11am-1am; 🛜)

Entertainment

Le Colisée   CINEMA

 23 Map p106, B3

The plushest cinema in town, Le Colisée, near Rue Mohammed el-Beqal, has Dolby sound and a mixed male-female, Moroccan and expat crowd. Films are sometimes in the original language (including English) and subtitled in French. (☑0524 44 88 93; Blvd Mohammed Zerktouni; orchestra/balcony Dh25/35)

Shopping

33 Rue Majorelle   FASHION

24 Map p106, D1

Over 60 designers, mostly from Morocco, are represented at 33 Majorelle, and co-owner Yehia Abdelnour dedicates much of his time to sourcing local *maâlems* (master artisans) who make the majority of what's on view. (☑0524 31 41 95; www.33ruemajorelle.com; 33 Rue Yves Saint Laurent; ⊙9.30am-7pm)

Ensemble Artisanal   ARTS, CRAFTS

25 Map p106, E5

To get a jump-start on the souqs, come to this government-sponsored showcase, across from Cyber Park, to glimpse master artisans at work and see the range of crafts and prices Marrakesh has to offer. The set prices are higher than in the souqs, but it's hassle-free shopping and the producer gets paid directly. (Ave Mohammed V; ⏰9.30am-12.30pm & 3-7pm Mon-Sat)

Darart Librairie BOOKS

26 Map p106, D1

This bookshop and cafe sells glossy coffee-table books about Morocco, with a small selection of English as well as French titles. There's also a tiny shelf of Morocco travel guidebooks and a decent clutch of Moroccan cookery books. Upstairs on the mezzanine level it serves coffee and teas. (☎0524 31 45 93; 79 Rue Yves Saint Laurent; ⏰9am-6pm)

Atika SHOES

27 Map p106, B3

With more colours than a sweet shop, Atika loafers are a Marrakesh must-have. Some customers have been known to buy their favourite shoe in 10 different colours, and at Dh650 to Dh700 a pair, a quarter of the price of designer-brand Tod's lookalikes, who can blame them? (☎0524 43 95 76; 34 Rue de la Liberté; ⏰8.30am-12.30pm & 3.30-8pm Mon-Sat)

Marché Ibn Toumert FOOD & DRINK

28 Map p106, C4

At this central market you'll find preserved lemons, spices and other

---

Local Life

Guéliz Sweet Treats

Care for a sweet? Sample Hakima Alami's sweet and savoury delicacies featuring figs, orange-flower water, desert honey and other local, seasonal ingredients at **Pâtisserie al-Jawda** (www.al-jawda.com; 11 Rue de la Liberté; ⏰8am-7.30pm; 🅿️ 🚻) if you want to explore the best of Marrakesh's deliciously sticky Moroccan sweet treats. For Viennoiserie and multi-coloured macarons check out **Pâtisserie Amandine** (☎0524 44 96 12; www.amandinemarrakech.com; 177 Rue Mohamed El Beqal; ⏰6am-11pm; ❄️ 🚻).

On a hot day ice-cream lovers should head straight to local favourite **Venezia Ice** (www.venezia-ice.com; train station, Ave Mohammed VI; ⏰9am-10pm; 🚻) for rich ice creams and tangy sorbets made by a Casablanca-based company.

---

food products at reasonable prices – if you're prepared to bargain a little. Plus there are a few stalls selling silver jewellery and hand-painted ceramics. (Rue ibn Toumert; ⏰8am-7pm)

L'Atelier du Vin WINE

29 Map p106, A2

For Moroccan wines at realistic prices, head to this dedicated wine shop; check the store's Facebook page for wine-tasting events. (☎0524 45 71 12; www.atelierduvin.ma; 87 Rue Mohamed el-Beqal; ⏰9.30am-12.30pm & 3.30-8pm Mon-Sat)

Top Sights
Palmeraie

Getting There

🚖 Taxi Most visitors hire taxis for a round-trip.

🚌 Marrakech City Tour (☎0663 52 77 97; www.alsa.ma; adult/child Dh145/75) This hop-on-hop-off bus does afternoon Palmeraie circuits.

If the tightly woven medina alleys are making you miss nature's wide spaces, escape to the Palmeraie. Wrapped up in the legends of Marrakesh's beginnings, this sweep of greenery is now the haunt of hotels and chi-chi holiday homes. Plenty of resorts here offer lunch-and-pool deals for a recuperating afternoon while quad-bike and dromedary rides through the palms offer a slice of desert fun.

Resort pool, Palmeraie

Don't Miss

Marrakesh's Green Lungs

So the legend goes, Marrakesh's *palmeraie* (palm grove) took root when the city's founding Berber army troops spat their date stones here. Today this shady haven, edging Marrakesh's northwest corner, contains roughly 50,000 date palms which help keep temperatures lower than in the central city. The five kilometre 'Palmeraie Circuit' is speckled with villas and luxury resorts.

Modern Art & Garden Strolls

In these adobe houses, the **Musée de la Palmeraie** (📞0661 09 53 52; Rte de Fez; adult/child Dh40/free; ⏱9.30am-5pm) displays a collection of Moroccan modern art that includes calligraphy, photography, painting and sculpture. Outside, though, is the real highlight. The museum's immaculate gardens (including a cacti garden and Andalucian garden) are a tranquil escape from the city.

Dromedary Rides

If you don't have time for a desert excursion, the Palmeraie has two dromedary stations where you can experience a **camel ride** (about Dh50 to Dh70, bargain hard) between the palms. Rides are about 45 minutes and are tailored towards complete novice camel-riders. If that all seems too sedate and scenic, the dromedary stations also offer quad bike (ATV) tours.

Saddling Up

For those who want to properly explore, **Les Cavaliers de L'Atlas** (📞0672 84 55 79; www.lescavaliersdelatlas.com; Rte de Casablanca; half day Dh350-565, full day Dh1000-1350) is a professional stable near the Palmeraie. It offers half- and full-day rides and has a mix of Arab, Anglo-Arab and Berber horses, as well as Shetland ponies for children.

Rte de Casablanca, 5km northwest of town

☑ Top Tips

▶ If you just want to peek at the palms and go for a dromedary ride, the hop-on-hop-off bus is the easiest transport option. There are hourly buses between 1pm and 5pm.

✕ Take a Break

Chill out at **Casa Taos** (📞0661 20 04 14; www.casataos.net; Km 8 Rte de Souihla; P ✱ 🛜 ≋) which offers lunch-and-pool packages to nonguests. For total relaxation, book a stay at serene **Jnane Tamsna** (📞0524 32 94 23; www.jnanetamsna.com; Douar Abiad, Palmeraie; d from Dh2800-3300, ste from Dh4000; ✱ @ ≋).

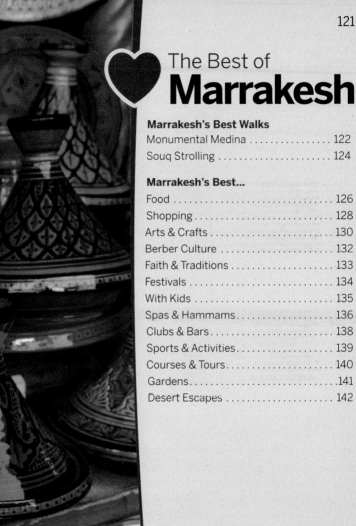

The Best of
Marrakesh

Hand-painted tajines
CHRIS HEPBURN/GETTY IMAGES ©

Best Walks
Monumental Medina

🏃 The Walk

Take a stroll down a Marrakesh memory lane and hit all of the city's major historic monuments in one swoop. These are the grand palaces and religious buildings – hidden behind high nondescript walls – that Marrakesh's sultans and pashas bequeathed on the pink-walled city to raise it into their imperial capital.

Start Ali ben Youssef Medersa

Finish Saadian Tombs

Length 4km; three hours

🍴 Take a Break

Marrakesh's main square **Djemaa el-Fna** (p24) is rimmed by cafes and restaurants where you can grab a bite or just a drink. Try **Café Kessabine** (p32) to munch on *pastilla* (rich savoury-sweet pie) or simply grab an orange juice from one of the square's juice stands.

Lazama Synagogue

❶ Ali ben Youssef Medersa

Step inside the **Ali ben Youssef Medersa** (p60) and find yourself surrounded by contemplative beauty that soothes away the distractions of the outside world. The joyful flurry of *zellij* (ceramic tile mosaic) and intricate carved wood here, though, must have provided ample distraction to students trying to study within this old religious seminary.

❷ Musée de Marrakech

The Mnebhi Palace was once was the stage for the highfalutin lifestyles of Marrakesh's rich and powerful, but now plays host to the **Musée de Marrakech** (p62), displaying both modern and ancient art exhibits.

❸ Koutoubia Mosque

With mathematically pleasing proportions, bestowed by its Almohad architects, the golden-hued stone minaret of the **Koutoubia Mosque** (p26) is the city's most recognisable sight.

❹ Dar Si Said

A rich riot of *zouak* (painted wood) work graces the ceilings of the first-floor salons in the **Dar Si Said** (p86), which is also home to the exhibits of the Museum of Moroccan Arts.

❺ Bahia Palace

It's not called *La Bahia* (the beautiful) for nothing. **Bahia Palace** (p82) is a triumphant vision of opulence created by Grand Vizier Si Moussa. The work on the cedar-wood ceilings is a masterful display of what can be achieved by Moroccan *mâalems* (master artisans).

❻ Mellah

Take a break from by-gone glitz and immerse yourself in Marrakesh's **mellah** (Jewish quarter), where the city's Jewish community once lived. As well as dipping into the tangle of alleyways, you can visit the **Lazama Synagogue** (p89) and the tombs of the **Miaâra Jewish Cemetery** (p89).

❼ Badi Palace

The 16th century **Badi Palace** (p89), once paved in gold, turquoise and crytal, now lies in jagged ruins, having been destroyed less than 100 years after al-Mansour ordered it to be built.

❽ Saadian Tombs

The **Saadian Tombs** (p84), where al-Mansour lies in rest, are an extravagance of marble and ornate plasterwork that showcase the Saadian era's flair for interior overkill.

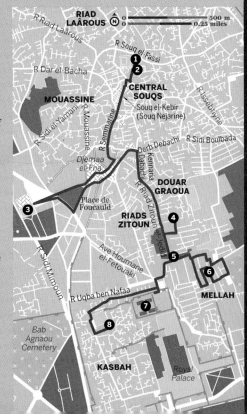

Best Walks
Souq Strolling

🏃 The Walk

Marrakesh is defined by its dawdling lanes of souqs, which bend and turn in what seems an unfathomable maze. It is the very core of this historic trading post, where caravans emerged from their long journeys to buy, sell and trade. Although travellers today arrive by plane and train, not camel, Marrakesh's long tradition of commerce and artisan work continues. Explore the bustling market streets, artisan quarters and pink-hued muddling alleys that make up the medina's centre.

Start Djemaa el-Fna

Finish Place Rahba Kedima

Length 2km; two hours

✖ Take a Break

In Mouassine both **Kafe Fnaque Berbère** (p53) and **Dar Cherifa** (p54) are welcoming places for a pot of tea and a snack while you consult your map, ready for further souq exploits.

Place Rahba Kedima

❶ Djemaa el-Fna

The best place to get your bearings ready for a souq-assault is **Djemaa el-Fna** (p24). Marrakesh's main square is the pumping heart of the medina with arteries of souqs threading out in all directions. The main entertainment here doesn't start thumping until dusk, but even in the day this place is a hive of energy.

❷ Rue Mouassine

Head north through Souq Ablueh (Olive Souq) and turn west onto Souq Quessabine until you hit the small square of Place Bab Fteuh. From here it's a straight (well as straight as a souq can be) stroll north on **Rue Mouassine**.

❸ Musée Douiria de Mouassine

The alley that leads behind the Mouassine Mosque is a narrow squiggle, tinted powder-puff pink. Follow it to **Musée Douiria de Mouassine** (p47) to view the jewel-coloured interior that has been painstakingly restored to its former glory.

❹ Souq Sebbaghine

Meander your way back to the mosque and dive head first into the souq streets to the north. **Souq Sebbaghine** is the dyer's souq. Check out the rainbow-haul of wool skeins swinging from the rafters and the pots of dye-powder sitting beside the cubby-hole workshops.

❺ Souq Haddadine

Souq Kchachbia is a mainline for souvenir shopping, but if you can pull yourself away from all that glitters and veer east you'll hit **Souq Haddadine** (Blacksmith's Souq; p67). The shops here are full of artisans at work and a good opportunity to buy direct from the producer.

❻ The Qissariat

Head onto Souq Smata and then get ready to lose your bearings slightly as you weave into the **qissariat** (covered markets). This warren of passages still hold onto its traditional feel.

A good place to bargain for *babouches* (leather slippers).

❼ Place Rahba Kedima

The *qissariat* alleys all join onto Souq el-Kebir from where it's only a short hop to **Place Rahba Kedima**. Hawkers on the central square sell handmade souvenirs while spice fans will appreciate the heady scents of cumin and cinnamon surrounding the apothecary stores here.

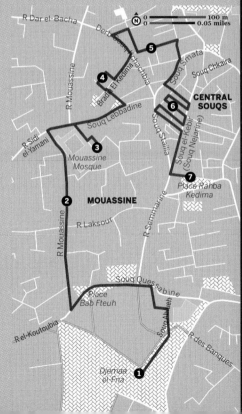

Best
Food

HUW JONES/GETTY IMAGES ©

Marrakesh has flown under the foodie-traveller radar for years but it's trying hard to play catch-up now. There's not a big local dining out culture which explains why so many restaurants can be hit-and-miss, serving up watery couscous and bland tajines. You need to dig a bit deeper to sample the hearty savoury-sweet flavours of real Marrakshi food.

Riad Dadas

The *dadas* (chefs) who work in the medina's riads are the unsung heroes of Marrakesh's culinary scene. Many riads open up their courtyard or roof-top restaurant to non-guests so you can sample different *dadas'* takes on Moroccan specialities. In nearly all cases, you have to book beforehand due to both limited seating and so the *dadas* can plan the menu in advance.

Snak Attack

The street-food scene is thriving in Marrakesh so don't be afraid to jump on in. Hard-working souq workers with no time for a long lazy lunch head to a *snak* (kiosk) to feast on peppery *merguez* (spicy lamb sausage), *teyhan* (stuffed spleen) and *brochettes* (kebabs). Join the queue at the one thronged with locals for the freshest, tastiest feeds.

Fusion Fad

French cuisine has always played a role in Marrakesh's modern culinary scene, but recently more restaurants are playing around with Middle Eastern, Italian and Spanish cooking traditions and merging them with Moroccan flavours. This Mediterranean fusion style can be a tasty break when you've eaten your fill of tajines.

☑ Top Tips

▶ Many restaurants offer *prix fixe* (three-course) lunch menus which are similar but better value than dinner menus.

▶ Top-end restaurants usually open between noon and 2.30pm and 7.30pm and 11pm.

▶ Alcohol is not widely available in medina restaurants.

▶ Reservations are recommended (and sometimes essential) for most top-end restaurants.

Left: Tanjia, a crock-pot stew cooked in the fire of a hammam **Above:** La Maison Arabe

Moroccan Just Like Mamma Makes It

Amal Centre Top lunchtime feasting on Moroccan home-cooking, plus you support a worthy cause just by eating. (p111)

Naíma Family-run restaurant that serves up superior couscous made fresh daily. (p75)

Riad Dining

Le Tobsil Bring a hearty appetite for the Moroccan five-course dinner extravaganza here. (p33)

La Maison Arabe The regal surroundings makes for a dinner with serious style-cred. (p51)

Foodie Treats

Al-Fassia Hands-down the best *mezze* (starter-size plates) in Marrakesh. (p110)

Gastro MK Book as far in advance as possible to experience this riad's innovative Moroccan-Mediterranean menu. (p33)

Like a Local

Mechoui Alley Slow-roasted lamb straight from the pit oven. Enough said. (p29)

Haj Mustapha The best place in town to dig into Marrakshi crock-pot speciality *tanjia* (slow-cooked stew). (p32)

Henna Café Get a henna tattoo and munch on *kefta* (meatball) sandwiches. All proceeds go to charity. (p45)

Sweet Treats

Pâtisserie al-Jawda Sweets, glorious sweets. (p117)

Panna Gelato Gives the Italians a run for their money. (p94)

Pâtisserie des Princes Pining for pain au chocolat? Head here. (p29)

International Flavours

PepeNero Come for house-made pasta, stay for succulent steak fillets. (p96)

Nomad The menu cherry-picks Mediterranean flavours and the rooftop is a chilled-out retreat. (p75)

Catanzaro Cracking wood-fired pizzas...comfort food for those far from home. (p111)

HEMIS/ALAMY ©

Best
Shopping

Think of the souqs as the medieval world's version of a shopping mall. Whether you want to spice up your pantry with some exotic flavours, buy a carpet to add Moroccan-wow to your living room, or invest in an it-bag that will have your friends drooling, this Aladdin's Cave of treasures is manna for shop-til-you-drop fanatics.

ALBERTO COTO/GETTY IMAGES ©

Souq Know-how

The main market streets are Souq Semmarine and Souq el-Kebir. If you see something you really like there, fine – but understand prices will be higher. Smaller souqs, and souqs dedicated to artisan workshops such as Souq Haddadine (Blacksmith's Souq), where you can buy direct off the producer, generally have the best deals. Wherever you decide to shop in the souqs, don't do it while grumpy or tired. To succeed at haggling you need to be in a good mood and see it as a bit of fun. Also, always remember that if you go into a shop with a guide then your price will be higher to cover his commission.

Carpets

Creiee Berbere is the carpet souq but you'll find carpet shops scattered throughout the city. Whatever you're dreaming could look great in your lounge, know your limits: namely, how much floor space you actually have. Tread cautiously with claims of antique carpets. New rugs are sometimes 'aged' by being stomped on or bleached by the sun. Also, understand what factors boost carpet value. Natural dyes and a higher number of knots per sq cm cost more.

Cooperative Shopping

Al Nour Fabulous hand-stitched household linens made by a collective of artisans with disabilities. (p37)

Assouss Cooperative d'Argane Gorgeous argan essential oils to slather over skin, sold by a women's cooperative. (p42)

Cooperative Artisanale des Femmes de Marrakesh Hand-crafted items by female *mâalems* (master artisans). (p56)

Al Kawtar Delicately embroidered textiles for bathrooms and kitchens; a business supporting disabled women. (p56)

CULTURA TRAVEL/ADIE BUSH/GETTY IMAGES ©

Artisan at work on a loom

Art & Crafts

Anamil A high-quality haul of ceramics, textiles and leatherware for those looking for something special. (p77)

Maison de la Photographie Take a bit of history home with you from the vintage photography selection here. (p64)

Funduq el Ouarzazi A magpie-horde of trinkets, jewellery, lamps and crafts jostle for attention in this ancient *funduq* (caraveneserai). (p37)

Modern Moroccan Design

Souk Cherifa Young designers pitch their claim on the upper-balcony salons here selling quirky accessories and homewares. (p43)

33 Rue Majorelle Master craftspeople create contemporary twists on traditional design. (p116)

Maktoub The medina goes hipster at this concept store. (p43)

Pop-up Shop Traditional Moroccan fashion gets a modern makeover. (p55)

Moroccan Beauty Products

Naturom Heavenly potions and lotions all fully organic and locally made. (p97)

L'Art du Bain Savonnerie Artisanale Luxurious soapy stuff. Great for gifts – if you succeed in not keeping them for yourself. (p43)

Worth a Trip

The industrial quarter of **Sidi Ghanem** (www.sidighanem.net) is located on Route de Safi, 4km outside Marrakesh. It is chock-full of design studios selling direct from their outlets. This is where to pick up modern spins on Moroccan ceramics and textiles as well as enough traditional artisan crafts and furniture to kit out your own riad.

Best
Arts & Crafts

Palaces are a riot of tilework detail, floral designs and swirling carved design, and riads are decked with intricate plasterwork. Marrakesh is a city steeped in ancient artistry and those traditions are kept alive by the modern craftspeople of the souqs and contemporary art scene of the Ville Nouvelle.

LONELY PLANET/GETTY IMAGES ©

Traditional Techniques

Brush up on craft know-how before you view Marrakesh's monuments or trawl the souqs for a slice of Moroccan artistry. *Zellij* is a mosaic of glazed tiles fitted into intricate geometric designs while *zouak* is a painted-wood technique used to high effect on door panels and cedar-wood ceilings.

In the souqs you'll see ceramic crafts from across Morocco, but you can stick local as Marrakesh specialises in monochrome ceramics in red, graphite and orange. For traditional textile techniques, look out for blue-and-white patterned *terz fezzi* linens and colourful silk Rabati embroidery. And keep your eyes peeled for *passementerie* (trims) *mâalems* (master artisans) at work, hand-spinning thread from a nail stuck in the souq wall to create silken tassels and knotted buttons.

Contemporary Art

Trail-blazing the way forward, Marrakesh is the centre of Morocco's small but growing modern-art scene. Marrakesh's contemporary artists combine elemental forms with organic, traditional materials, helping to ground abstract art in Morocco as an indigenous art form. The scene has taken off in the past decade with the Marrakech Biennale (www.marrakechbiennale.com) launched in 2005 and the Ville Nouvelle is now home to several art galleries.

☑ **Top Tips**

▶ Morrocan ceramics are excellent value – a decorative tajine may run you Dh150 to Dh400, depending on size and decoration, making this a great piece of local craftwork to take home. Be aware, though, that most decorative tajines are not oven-safe and are for ornamental use only.

A lamp-maker works on his craft

Craftspeople at Work

Ensemble Artisanal
Head here for a gander at local craftspeople and artisans at work. (p116)

Souq Haddadine
The medina's black-smiths have their work-shops here. (p67)

Galleries

Galerie Ré Check out the city's funkiest contemporary art space. (p105)

Dar Bellarj Old stork hospital converted into a gallery devoted to promoting local art heritage. (p71)

Matisse Art Gallery
Small but internationally renowned gallery showing work by some of Morocco's best-known artists. (p104)

Masterful Artisan Interiors

Bahia Palace Tip your hat to the *mâalems* who worked their magic over the lush interiors of this opulent old regal residence. (p82)

Ali ben Youssef Medersa
Inspired craftsmanship makes this one of North Africa's most beautiful old *medersas* (theological colleges). (p60)

Saadian Tombs An interior that was worth dying for. (p84)

Unusual Crafts

Creations Pneumatiques Collect your sustainable-art brownie points here with recycled tyre-tread crafts. (p98)

Michi Gifts made from recycled goods, such as flour-sack *babouches* (slippers) and oil-drum mirrors. (p43)

Best
Berber Culture

KERRY DUNSTONE/ROBERT HARDING ©

Marrakesh has Amazigh (Berber) roots, founded by the tribes of the Atlas Mountains who became the Almoravid dynasty. Through its long history this city has kept up its Berber connection, functioning over the centuries as a vital commercial hub where Amazigh tribes came to buy and sell. These associations remain strong and Berber culture is alive and well in Marrakesh.

Berber Folk Music

To experience a slice of Berber culture while you're in Marrakesh, catch a Berber folk-music performance.

Berber music uses a minimum of accompanying instruments, usually depending on a drum to set the rhythm and the flute to carry the tune. Because of the huge diversity of different Amazigh tribes, there is a rich breadth of musical styles under the Berber umbrella.

The Marrakech Festival of Popular Arts (p134) is a great time to be in the city if you want to catch a variety of Berber folk-music groups. At other times, head to Djemaa el-Fna in the evening. On any given night the square plays host to some Berber musicians.

Berber Museum Don't miss this stunning collection of Berber artefacts, art, textiles and jewellery at Jardin Majorelle. (p102)

Djemaa el-Fna Among the snake-charmers and soothsayers you'll find Berber musicians entertaining the crowds in the evenings (p54)

Maison Tiskiwin Berber artefacts and craftwork take prime position in anthropologist Bert Flint's collection of indigenous crafts. (p90)

Cafe Clock Every Sunday night from 6pm this cafe in the kasbah area hosts Amazigh bands. (p94)

Musée Boucharouite Berber rag-rugs take centre stage at this popular art museum highlighting lesser-known crafts. (p71)

Dar Si Said Leatherware and textiles of the Berber peoples make up part of the museum collection here. (p86)

Best
Faith & Traditions

You'll understand how religion permeates the rhythms of daily life when you hear the sonorous call to prayer echo out from the mosques. As an old imperial capital, Marrakesh is home to some beautiful examples of Islamic religious architecture, but it also holds on to a heritage of other religious communities who once made this city a vibrant caravan town.

KEVIN FOY/ALAMY ©

Things to Remember

If this is your first visit to a Muslim country you may wonder how this will affect your trip. The main point is, it won't. Sunday is the official day off for shops and banks although on Fridays (the Muslim holy day) you'll find some souq shops closed, particularly in the traditional workshop areas.

Alcohol is freely available in restaurants, bars and supermarkets in the Ville Nouvelle, although due to expensive alcohol licenses it is harder to source in the medina. If you're travelling during Ramadan (the Muslim holy month of fasting) you won't be expected to observe the fast but should refrain from eating and smoking in public during daylight.

Koutoubia Mosque The golden stone Koutoubia minaret is the landmark of the city. (p26)

Miaâra Tranquil, sprawling Jewish cemetery (pictured above) on the edge of the atmospheric cramped alleyways of the *mellah* (Jewish quarter). (p89)

Koutoubia Minbar Spectacular prayer pulpit now residing at Badi Palace. (p89)

Ali ben Youssef Medersa This religious seminary is one of Morocco's best examples of Islamic art. (p60)

☑ Top Tips

▶ Wear clothing that covers shoulders and knees while in the medina, to respect older, and more traditional, Moroccans.

▶ If someone greets you with *es salaam alaykum* (peace be upon you), reply with *wa alaykum salaam* (and upon you, be peace).

▶ Non-Muslims cannot enter any of Marrakesh's mosques or religious shrines.

Best
Festivals

Marrakesh hosts an annual program of festivals befitting its self-proclaimed role as Morocco's cultural capital. From contemporary art and film to traditional song and dance, Marrakesh loves to get its glad rags on and play host. Tickets to events can generally be bought beforehand through festival websites or at official ticket outlets in town.

SERGIO PITAMITZ/GETTY IMAGES ©

Marrakech Festival of Popular Arts (www.marrakechfestival.com; ⏲Jul) The only thing hotter than Marrakesh in July is this free-form folk festival. Berber musicians, dancers and street performers from around the country pour into Marrakesh to thrill the masses. Most of the action takes place amid the ruins of Badi Palace, giving a regal backdrop to the proceedings.

Marrakech Biennale (www.marrakechbiennale.org; ⏲Feb) Promoting debate and dialogue through artistic exchange, this major trilingual (Arabic, French and English) festival invites local and international artists to create literary, artistic, architectural and digital works throughout the city. Held every other year (even years).

Marrakech International Film Festival (www.festivalmarrakech.info; ⏲Dec) Stars from Hollywood to Bollywood strut the Berber red carpet at this week-long festival, culminating in wildly unpredictable awards shows.

Marrakech Marathon (www.marathon-marrakech.com; half-/full-marathon fee €30/50; ⏲Jan) Run like there's a carpet salesman after you from the Djemaa to the Palmeraie and back for this annual marathon.

TEDx Marrakesh (www.tedxmarrakesh.net; day/weekend Dh700/800; ⏲Sep) Like any self-respecting cultural capital, Marrakesh has its own TEDx talkfest, where Marrakshi movers and shakers take on challenging themes such as 'Driving Forces' and 'Dare to Question'.

MadJazz (www.madjazz-festival.com; ⏲Mar) Marrakesh invents new sounds nightly with Gnawa castanets, jazz riffs and Jimi Hendrix guitar licks.

Jardin'Art (⏲mid-Apr) Celebrate Marrakesh in bloom mid-April, with temporary gardens, garden-inspired art shows, botanical talks and displays.

Best
With Kids

The mutual admiration between kids and Marrakesh is obvious. They'll gaze in wonderment at souq scenes, snake charmers serenading cobras and herbalists trading concoctions straight from a scene in *Harry Potter*. That said, for families with toddlers and babies, the city can be overwhelming and logistically challenging. Planning, and careful accommodation selection, takes the stress out of visiting Marrakesh with younger children.

PETER PHIPP/GETTY IMAGES ©

Riad Plusses & Minuses

The key to a successful trip is child-friendly accommodation. Fair warning: riad plunge pools and steep stairs aren't exactly child-proof, and sound reverberates through riad courtyards. Most riad owners and staff, however, dote on babies and will provide cots and high chairs, and cater special meals on request.

Entertainment That Costs Nothing

Marrakesh museums are a poor substitute for the live theatre of the souqs and the Djemaa

el-Fna. Early mornings are quieter in the souqs, meaning less hassle and a better view of crafts-people at work. Early evening (6pm to 8pm) are best for Djemaa storytellers and offer chance encounters with Moroccan families also doing the rounds.

Beldi Country Club

(📞0524 38 39 50; http://beldicountryclub.com; Km6 Rte de Barrage 'Cherifa'; adult/child incl lounger & lunch Dh370/250; 🏊) A 15-hectare country retreat designed with families in mind; includes two children's pools and activities ranging from cycling to pottery workshops.

Terres d'Amanar (📞0524 43 81 03; www.terresdamanar.com; Douar Akli, Tahanaoute; activities from Dh100) For active kids: learn to master zip-lines, river-rafting, BMX cycling and donkey polo. It's located 36km south of Marrakesh.

Oasiria (📞0524 38 04 38; www.oasiria.com; Km 4, Rte d'Amizmiz; adult Dh130, child 0.80-1.5m Dh90, child under 0.80m free; 🕙10am-6pm) All-day family fun whizzing down kamikaze and cobra slides and playing in wave pools and pirate lagoons.

Best
Spas & Hammams

MARKA/ALAMY ©

The quintessential Moroccan experience. After dusty sightseeing exploits a good scrubbing leaves you squeaky clean, fresh and invigorated to take on the medina again. Public hammams are not for the faint of heart but are great for local interaction. The city's flourishing private hammam scene allows the less adventurous a more refined and relaxing experience.

Bathing Rituals

A hammam at its simplest is a steam bath where you wash yourself down, sweat out the dirt of the day and then scrub, with an optional massage afterwards. For many Moroccans hammams are as much a social occasion (particularly for women) as they are about bathing. If you're going to go local with a public hammam be aware that a few public hammams don't accept non-Muslims. It's best to ask for hammam recommendations from locals.

Hammam History

Public baths were first introduced to Morocco (and the rest of North Africa) by the Romans and adapted to fit in with Islamic ablution rituals – foregoing the communal Roman bathing pool to use running water to wash under instead – after Islam gained a foothold across the region.

What Happens, Where

Hammams are made up of three interconnected areas: the *caldarium* (hot room), the *tepidarium* (warm room) and the *frigidarium* (cool room). You sweat the dirt out and *gommage* (scrub) in the steamy hot room, sluice yourself down with buckets of water in the warm room, and relax afterwards in the cool room.

☑ Top Tips

▸ It's best to book ahead for private hammams, and couples need to reserve a private session if they want to experience a hammam together.

▸ Public hammams are usually open for women during the day and men during the evening, though there are some exceptions to the rule.

Sultana Spa

Public Hammams

Hammam Dar el-Bacha
The best option if you want to go for a fully local public hammam experience. (p50)

Hammam Bab Doukkala
A historic public hammam dating from the 17th century. Good local choice for male travellers. (p50)

Midrange Private Hammams

Medina Spa Private hammam with friendly staff known for great massages. (p29)

Hammam Ziani Less spruced-up than other hammams, but has super-friendly female masseurs. Good choice for female travellers. (p92)

Private Hammam-spas

Le Bain Bleu Super stylish surroundings and luxurious spa-like services. Go on, treat yourself. (p48)

Heritage Spa This private hammam offers rejuvenating deep-cleaning treatments. Great choice for couples. Professional staff. (p48)

Sultana Spa Pampering treatments and massage packages for couples at this splendid marble-clad private hammam. (p91)

Le Jardins de la Medina Indulge in some spa treatments at this chic boutique hotel in the kasbah. (p91)

Best
Clubs & Bars

LONELY PLANET/GETTY IMAGES ©

Marrakesh doesn't have a huge nightlife scene, but there is a scattering of bars and clubs, particularly in the Ville Nouvelle, that are worth checking out for a night on the town. Saturday night is the best time for clubbing fans – other days tend to be much quieter.

Drinking in the Medina

The medina only has a handful of restaurants and bars officially serving alcohol, although many riads sell beer and wine to guests in the privacy of their courtyard gardens. Restaurants that serve alcohol are generally fine for you to come in just for a drink.

Café Arabe Head here for cocktails as the sun sets over the medina. (p53)

Djellabar Crazy pop-art interiors and the cocktail menu is the best in town. (p113)

Kechmara Bar-restaurant with an arty vibe and good music that attracts a fun crowd. (p105)

Kosybar Chill out with a beer while watching the storks preen themselves on the ancient ramparts. (p97)

Café du Livre Cosy cafe-bar with friendly staff, draught beer, board games and strong cocktails. (p112)

Piano Bar Refined riad surroundings with a jazz-soundtrack for a quiet drink to top off the day. (p34)

Comptoir An extravaganza of Marrakshi hipsters when it's pumping, with belly-dancers thrown in for good measure. (p116)

Churchill Bar Historic bar once host to certain world leaders. Prices are eye-watering. (p115)

Theatro Marrakesh's most dependable club for a big night out, complete with hilarious floor shows. (p115)

☑ Top Tips

▶ Most clubs charge entry fees ranging from Dh150 to Dh350, including the first drink, but midweek those who arrive early and dress smartly may get in free.

▶ You have to be a night-owl to sample Marrakesh's club scene. Most clubs don't kick off until after midnight.

Best
Sports &
Activities

Action Sport Loisirs

(📞0661 24 01 45; www.
marrakechbikeaction.
com; Apt 4, 2nd fl, Ave
Yacoub el-Mansour; half-day
Dh300-350, full-day Dh750)
Organises cycling circuits
of the Palmeraie and
Marrakesh gardens and
longer excursions to the
Ourika Valley and Lalla
Takerkoust with lunch
included.

Fellah Hotel

(📞0525
06 50 00; www.fellah-hotel.
com; Km 13 Rte de l'Ourika,
Tassoultante; d from Dh1900;
P ❄ 🛜 🏊) This hotel –
part spa-resort, part
cultural-hub and commu-
nity outreach program –
defies easy definitions.
The on-site **Dar al
Ma'mûm Foundation art
centre** hosts a program
of cultural activities that
non-guests can attend
and you can also feel the
love by booking in for
lunch or Sunday brunch
(Dh250).

Inside Morocco Travel

(📞0524 43 00 20; www.
insidemoroccotravel.com;
4th fl, 29 Rue de Yougoslavie;
🕐9am-noon & 3-7pm Mon-
Sat) Bespoke adventures
designed for you by eco-
tourism expert Mohamed
Nour and his multilingual
team – sunset tea for
two in the Sahara, hikes
off-the-beaten track in
the Zat and Ouirgane
valleys, home cooking in
Berber mountain villages
and crafts workshops
with inspiring women's
cooperatives.

Morocco Adventure &
Rafting

(📞0614 97 23 16;
www.rafting.ma; Rue Beni
Marine; per person £1150)
This company has been
leading rafting expedi-
tions in the Atlas Moun-
tains for over 12 years
with a team of local and
international guides, all
with a minimum of five
years guiding experience.
Excursions range from

half-day trips to Ourika
to a week-long excursion
in the Ahansal valley, a
highlight of any trip.

Riad Bledna

(📞0661 18
20 90; www.riadbledna.com;
2km Route de Ouarzazate;
per person, incl lunch &
transfer Dh250; 🚴) This
4-acre organic garden
retreat is in a quiet Marrakesh suburb east of
the city centre. Day rates
cover use of the oxygen-
filtered pool, tasty
homemade lunches and
transfers to and from the
Djemaa el-Fna.

Best
Courses & Tours

OLIVER CIRENDINI/GETTY IMAGES ©

Souk Cuisine (📞0673 80 49 55; www.soukcuisine. com; Zniquat Rahba, 5 Derb Tahtah; per day incl meal & wine Dh520) Learn to cook as the *dadas* (chefs) do: shop in the souq for ingredients with English-speaking Dutch hostess Gemma van de Burgt, work alongside two Moroccan *dadas*, then enjoy the four-course lunch you helped cook. Courses are two-person minimum, 12 participants maximum; vegetarian courses possible.

Marrakech Food Tour (www.marrakechfoodtours. com; US$60; ⏰1pm & 6pm daily) Munch your way through the medina. Weave through the souqs tucking into *tanjia* (slow-cooked stew), sampling Marrakshi street food and slurping down avocado milkshakes. Hosts Youssef and Amanda take guests on a whirlwind tour of Marrakshi

flavours. Bring your appetite.

Creative Interactions (📞0524 42 26 87; www. creative-interactions.com; Imm. El Khalil Bldg, Apt 47, Ave Hassan II; 1½ hr private/ group €40/35, 3 hr private/ group €65/60) Moroccan Arabic classes designed for short-stay travellers. These fun and friendly workshops allow even travellers on a very short stay a chance to learn the basics they'll most need on their visit. A fantastic idea for those who want to dive a little further into Marrakshi culture on their trip.

Bled Al-Fassia (📞0524 32 96 60; www.alfassia. com; Rte de Fez, Douar Sidi Mbarek) Learn the secrets of the chefs behind Al-Fassia restaurant in the spotless stainless-steel kitchen of a luxury villa on the outskirts of Marrakesh. Rates available on request.

Desir du Maroc (📞0661 16 35 85; www.desirdumaroc. com) Marrakshi Abdelhay Sadouk has 30 years' experience leading history and culture tours around Marrakesh's lesser-known sites.

Mountain Voyage (📞0524 42 19 96; www. mountain-voyage.com; 2nd fl, Immeuble El Batoul, 5 Ave Mohammed V; ⏰9am-12.30pm & 3.30-7pm Mon-Sat) Organises tailor-made Marrakesh tours with English-speaking guides as well as multi-day excursions.

Best
Gardens

Outside of the medina's dense confines, Marrakesh is a surprisingly green city of vast gardens, many of which were once the exclusive domain of royalty. Many of the parks are fine relaxing territory so join the Marrakshis who come here to picnic, take an early-evening stroll or just beat the heat within their shady confines.

HUW JONES/GETTY IMAGES ©

Royal Parks

Marrakesh's largest parks are the Menara Gardens, southwest of the Ville Nouvelle, and the Agdal Gardens, southeast of the kasbah. Note that the entries to both are a good half hour walk (45 minutes to Agdal) from Djemaa el-Fna, and although vast, most of the space is taken up with scrubby olive groves. Nevertheless, both boast reflective pools which provide each park's focal point and are a popular hang-out spot for local families and courting couples on the weekend.

In summary, unless you're really into olive groves, the more central gardens are a much better bet if you're looking for a spot of chill-out time from the medina.

Jardin Majorelle Beautiful garden, once owned by Yves Saint Laurent and home to the Berber Museum. (p102)

Koutoubia Gardens The closest green space to the medina, with shady palm trees and manicured flower beds. (p29)

CyberPark Take a break between the medina and the Ville Nouvelle in this tranquil, pretty garden. (p108)

☑ Top Tips

▶ You can rent a calèche (horse-drawn carriage) from near Djemaa el-Fna to take you to Jardin Majorelle.

Musée de la Palmeraie Peaceful cacti and Andulucian gardens stretch behind this contemporary art gallery in the Palmeraie. (p119)

La Mamounia Gardens The La Mamounia Hotel's historic garden where Churchill once relaxed with his paint brushes. (p108)

Best
Desert Escapes

The rough, dry moon-like expanse of the Agafay Desert is only 40km southwest of Marrakesh down the Rte d'Amizmiz. This is a favoured playground for weekending Marrakshis who come for dune-gazing and canoeing on Lalla Takerkoust, a man-made reservoir. Take a break from city-life with an overnight trip here to catch a glimpse of Morocco's rawly beautiful natural scenery.

PAMELA VALENTE PHOTOGRAPHY/GETTY IMAGES ©

Scarabeo (✆0661 44 41 58; www.scarabeo-camp.com; standard/ste/child tent incl half board Dh2020/2580/1240) This nomadic eco-camp moves its 12 elegant bivouacs according to season, but there are always views of the desert and High Atlas. During the day spend your time trekking, riding camels, paragliding or flying kites and by night dozens of lamps light your way to open-air film projections and unforgettable stargazing.

La Pause (✆0661 30 64 94; www.lapause-marrakech.com; N 31°26.57, W 008°10.31, Douar Lmih Laroussiéne; per person incl full board Dh1685; ⌖) Skip off the grid to this desert getaway for days spent playing turf-free golf, throwing a frisbee about or hanging out in hammocks by the pool. Ride off into the sunset on mountain bikes, Arabian stallions or dromedaries and return to candlelit feasts.

Jnane Tihihit (✆0668 46 55 45; www.riad-t.com/jnane-tihihit; Douar Makhfamane; d Dh500-850; P⌖) Relax in whitewashed bungalows amid pomegranate trees. Foodies can tend saffron gardens and learn to make couscous while others can slip into lounge mode, relaxing by the pool or hanging out at the lakefront beach.

Dar Zitoune (✆0662 40 83 80; www.dar-zitoune.com; Douar Zii; s Dh480-530, d Dh660-810; P❋⌖) This stone-walled country house is a refuge from urban hustle. Host Anouar organises eco-excursions from canoeing and camel riding to trekking on the Kik Plateau.

Survival Guide

Survival Guide

Before You Go

When to Go

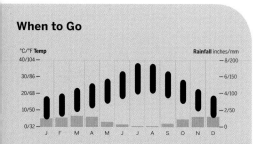

°C/°F Temp
40/104 —
30/86 —
20/68 —
10/50 —
0/32 —

Rainfall inches/mm
— 8/200
— 6/150
— 4/100
— 2/50
— 0

J F M A M J J A S O N D

➡ **Winter (Dec-Feb)**
Plenty of blue sky but extremely chilly at night. Riad rates pushed up between 20 December and 6 January.

➡ **Spring (Mar-May)**
Great time for medina escapades with temperatures hovering around 30°C. Avoid Easter holidays when prices jump.

➡ **Summer (June-Aug)**
Low season with scorching heats. Riad bargains aplenty and the Festival of Popular Arts hits town.

➡ **Autumn (Sep-Nov)**
Ideal weather for sightseeing and souq exploration.

Book Your Stay

☑ **Top Tip** Light sleepers should be aware that sound travels easily in riads and you're never too far from a mosque minaret in the medina. Bring earplugs to mute slamming doors and the early morning call to prayer, or choose a hotel in the Ville Nouvelle.

➡ Marrakesh is famous for its riad accommodation. These medina guesthouses have limited space so it's advisable to book in advance.

➡ Groups of friends or families travelling together can often book an entire riad to themselves.

➡ Book a month ahead if you want to visit Marrakesh during any major European holiday.

➡ There is no shortage of budget-friendly inns and guesthouses. Cheap hotels line Rue Sidi Bouloukat, south of Djemaa el-Fna between Rue Bab

Agnaou and Rue Riad Zitoun el Kedim.

➡ Brand-name luxury resorts sit on the outskirts of town. The Palmeraie is home to more intimate luxury villa guesthouses.

➡ Many riads and luxury hotels lower their prices mid-June to August, mid-January to mid-March and mid-November to mid-December.

Useful Websites

Marrakech & Beyond (www.marrakechandbeyond. com) Locally based English-Moroccan travel agency who can book riads and guesthouses, plus guides and activities.

Hip Marrakech (www. hipmarrakech.com) Travel company with wide selection of characterful riads in a variety of price ranges.

Marrakech Riads (www. marrakech-riads.com) Specialises in booking riad accommodation.

Lonely Planet (www. lonelyplanet.com) Author recommendation reviews and online booking.

Best Budget

Equity Point Hostel (www.equity-point.com) Historic riad features without the price tag.

Hotel du Trésor (www. hotel-du-tresor.com) Small, chic riad featuring arty flourishes. A short hop from Djemaa el-Fna.

Hôtel Toulousain (www. hoteltoulousain.com) Easygoing hotel in a prime Guéliz location.

Hôtel Atlas (www.hotel-atlas-marrakech.com) Cosy inn with rooms surrounding a leafy courtyard.

Best Midrange

Riad Le J (www.riadlej. com) Modern Italian style meets Marrakshi craftsmanship at this super funky riad.

Riad Wo (www.riadw.com) Minimalist Mallorcan chic makes Riad Wo a medina haven.

Dar Attajmil (www. darattajmil.com) Relaxed riad living with attentive staff and simple but sleek rooms.

Dar Zaman (www. darzaman.com) Bright and breezy design and extraordinary service make Dar Zaman stand out from the crowd.

Riad Magellan (www. riadmagellan.com) Hip hideaway behind the Mouassine Fountain.

Marhbabikoum (www. marhbabikoum.com) 'Marhbabikoum' means welcome and this mellow riad lives up to its name.

Best Top End

Dar Housnia (www. dar-housnia.com) Tradition and modernity blend seamlessly at this ultra-swish riad.

Tchaikana (www.tchaikana. com) Nomadic artefacts combine with swish contemporary design.

Jnane Tamsa (www. jnanetamsa.com) Sustainable style never looked so good at this Palmeraie resort.

Riad Al Massarah (www.riadalmassarah.com) Elegance with green credentials. The ultimate feel-good getaway.

Arriving in Marrakesh

....

☑ **Top Tip** For the best way to get to your accommodation, see p16.

Menara Airport

Most visitors arrive at **Menara Airport** (RAK; ☎0524 44 79 10; http:// marrakech.airport-authority. com; ⏰information desk 8am-6pm), 6km southwest of town.

➡ A petit taxi (local taxi) into Marrakesh from the airport should be no more than Dh100 but you may have difficulty convincing the driver of this.

➡ Airport transfers pre-arranged with your hotel are a good idea to avoid arrival hassle and aid navigation issues if you're staying in the medina.

➡ Pre-arranged airport transfers usually cost Dh170 to Dh250.

➡ Airport Bus No 19 (Dh30) departs every half hour between 6.15am and 9.45pm from outside the arrivals hall. It drops passengers at Djemaa el-Fna and near Place du 16 Novembre (in the Ville Nouvelle).

Marrakesh Train Station

The **Marrakesh Train Station** (☎0524 447768; cnr Ave Hassan II & Blvd Mohammed VI) is centrally located in Guéliz.

➡ Petit taxi drivers waiting at the station usually quote high fare rates (and don't use their meters).

➡ Hail a taxi off the street to get a better rate.

➡ Most hotels can arrange a driver to pick you up from the station.

➡ City bus Nos 8, 10 and 66 pick up passengers near the train station on Ave Hassan II and stop off at Bab Doukkala and Place de Foucauld (near Djemaa el-Fna).

CTM Bus Station

The **CTM Main bus station** (☎0524 43 44 02; www.ctm.ma; Rue Abou Bakr Seddiq; ⏰6am-10pm) is southwest of the train station. Some buses also stop at the Bab Douk-kala **bus station** (☎0524 433933) just outside the medina walls.

➡ Petits taxis hang around the bus station but you're better off walking up to Ave Hassan II and hailing off the street.

➡ Catch city bus Nos 8, 10 or 66 to the medina from Ave Hassan II.

➡ From the Bab Douk-kala bus station it's a 20-minute walk to Djemaa el-Fna.

Getting Around

....

Bus
☑ **Best for...** Local travel

➡ Useful for short hops between Djemaa el-Fna and the Ville Nouvelle.

➡ Bus Nos 1, 8, 10, 14, 16 and 66 all travel between Place de Foucauld, near Djemaa el-Fna and the Ville Nouvelle.

➡ Marrakesh city buses can get extremely crowded and very hot during summer.

➡ City bus tickets cost Dh4 one way.

➡ For more information see www.alsa.ma.

Calèche
☑ **Best for...** Scenic rides

➡ These horse-drawn green carriages congregate at Place de Foucauld, next to Djemaa el-Fna's southern exit.

➡ State-fixed rates of Dh120 per hour apply (rates are posted inside the carriage).

➡ Expect a tour of the ramparts to take 1½ hours.

➡ Avoid Marrakesh traffic rush hours (8am, noon and 5.30pm to 7.30pm).

Car & Motorcycle
☑ **Best for...** Exploring further afield.

➡ Hiring a car is useful for day excursions to the Agafay Desert or destinations such as Ourika and Ouirgane.

➡ Car parks near the medina are by the Koutoubia Mosque and just south of Place de Foucauld on Ave el-Mouahidine.

➡ Car park fees are usually Dh20 during the day, Dh40 for 24 hours.

➡ If you park on the street a guardian will expect a Dh10 tip for keeping an eye on your car.

Taxi
☑ **Best for...**
Convenience

➡ Marrakesh has a multitude of creamy-beige petits taxis.

➡ You can hail off the street or hire from a rank.

➡ Taxi journeys around town should never cost more than Dh20 during the day or Dh30 at night.

Essential Information

Business Hours
☑ **Top Tip** Some of medina souq shops close all day or for half a day on Friday, but are open all day on Sunday.

➡ Although a Muslim country, for business purposes Morocco follows the Monday to Friday working week.

➡ Friday is the main prayer day. Many businesses take an extended lunch break on Friday afternoon.

➡ During Ramadan the rhythm of the city changes, and office hours shift to around 10am to 3pm or 4pm.

Non-standard hours are listed in reviews; standard hours are as follows:

Banks 8.30am to 6.30pm Monday to Friday

Post offices 8.30am to 4.30pm Monday to Friday

Government offices 8.30am to 6.30pm Monday to Friday

Restaurants noon to 3pm and 7pm to 10pm

Bars 4pm till late

Shops 9am to 12.30pm and 2.30pm to 8pm Monday to Saturday (often closed longer at noon for prayer)

Tourist office 8.30am to noon and 2.30pm to 6.30pm Monday to Thursday, 8.30am to 11.30am and 3pm to 6.30pm Friday

Marrakech City Tour Bus
☑ **Best for...** Travellers with little time

➡ A hop-on-hop-off, open-top bus with two scenic city circuits.

➡ Buses leave every half hour between 9am and 6pm.

➡ Tickets can be bought at the Place de Foucauld bus stop.

Electricity

127V/220V/50Hz

127V/220V/50Hz

Emergency

Ambulance ☏150

Brigade Touristique
(☏0524 38 46 01; Rue Sidi
Mimoun; ⊙24hr)

Fire ☏150

Police (☏19; Rue Ouadi
el-Makhazine)

Polyclinique du Sud
(☏0524 44 79 99; cnr Rues
de Yougoslavie & Ibn Aicha;
⊙24hr) Private hospital
for serious cases and
emergency dental care.

Money

☑ **Top Tip** Break big
dirham notes whenever
possible. Moroccans
guard their small change
jealously and so should
you. The Dh20 note is the
most useful note in your
wallet.

➡ Moroccan dirham (Dh)
notes come in denomi-
nations of Dh20, Dh50,
Dh100 and Dh200.

➡ Dirham coins come in
denominations of Dh1,
Dh2, Dh5 and Dh10.

➡ The dirham is divided
into 100 centimes. You
may infrequently see cen-
time coins in denomina-
tions of 10, 20 and 50
centimes.

➡ The dirham is a
restricted currency, meaning that it cannot be taken
out of the country and is
not available abroad.

➡ Hang on to all exchange
receipts. You'll need
them to convert leftover
dirham at banks or
exchange bureaus before
you leave.

ATMs

➡ Virtually all ATMs
(guichets automatiques)
accept Visa, MasterCard,
Electron, Cirrus, Maestro
and InterBank cards.

➡ Most ATMs will
dispense no more than
Dh2000 at a time.

➡ ATMs habitually run
dry over the weekend,
particularly on Sundays.

➡ In the medina there are
ATMs around Djemaa
el-Fna and Place Kedima
Rahba.

➡ The Ville Nouvelle has
several ATMs along Ave
Mohammed V.

Cash

➡ The medina souqs are
still very much a cash
society. Only larger shops
will accept credit and
debit cards.

➡ Many midrange and top-end hotels and riads accept payment in euros.

Credit Cards

➡ Major credit cards are widely accepted at midrange and top-end accommodation, and large tourist-oriented restaurants and shops.

➡ Credit cards often attract a surcharge of around 5%.

Money Changers

➡ Euros, US dollars and British pounds are the most easily exchanged currencies.

➡ Most banks change cash. Large branches in the Ville Nouvelle will usually change travellers cheques if you bring your passport along.

Tipping in Marrakesh

SERVICE	TIP
Restaurant	10%
Cafe	Dh2
Museum guides	Dh3-5
Porters	Dh3-5
Public-toilet attendants	Dh1-2
Baggage handlers	Dh3-5
Petrol-pump attendants	Dh3-5
Car park attendants	Dh3-5; Dh10 for overnight parking

➡ Private exchange bureaus offer official exchange rates and are open longer hours but may charge commission.

Tipping

➡ Tipping is an integral part of Moroccan life; almost any service can warrant a tip.

➡ Don't be railroaded, but the judicious distribution of a few dirham for a service willingly rendered can make your life a lot easier.

Public Holidays

☑ **Top Tip** Alcohol is still available in Marrakesh during Ramadan in the Ville Nouvelle's restaurants and bars.

Dos & Don'ts

➡ Do always ask before taking a photo of locals.

➡ Don't drink alcohol on the street or in public spaces.

➡ Do cover knees and shoulders, whether you're a man or woman; it shows your respect for your Moroccan hosts.

➡ Don't eat in public during Ramadan.

➡ Do learn basic greetings. A few words in Darija (Moroccan Arabic) will delight your hosts.

➡ Don't skip pleasantries. Always say hello before asking for help or prices.

Banks, post offices and most shops shut on the main public holidays, although transport still runs.

New Year's Day 1 January.

Independence Manifesto 11 January – commemorates the publication in Fez of the Moroccan nationalist manifesto for independence.

Labour Day 1 May.

Feast of the Throne 30 July – commemorates King Mohammed VI's accession to the throne.

Allegiance of Oued Eddahab 14 August – celebrates the 'return to the fatherland' of the Oued Eddahab region in the far south.

Anniversary of the King's and People's Revolution 20 August – commemorates the exile of Mohammed V by the French in 1953.

Young People's Day 21 August – celebrates the king's birthday.

Anniversary of the Green March 6 November – commemorates the Green March 'reclaiming' the Western Sahara on November 1975.

Independence Day 18 November – commemorates independence from France.

Safe Travel

☑ **Top Tip** If you're lost in the medina ask a shopkeeper for directions. Often bored youths will point you the wrong way on purpose.

➡ Pickpockets work on Djemaa el-Fna and, to a lesser extent, around the medina. Keep your wits about you and carry only the minimum amount of cash necessary.

➡ Be particularly vigilant if walking around the medina at night.

Hustlers

➡ Hustlers and unofficial guides hang around the medina, often 'recommending' restaurants and shops to visitors.

➡ Hustlers are often desperate to make a living and can be persistent and sometimes unpleasant.

➡ Be aware that their main interest is usually gaining commission from the restaurant, hotel or shop that they have guided you to.

➡ Maintain your good humour and be polite when declining offers of help and the hassle tends to lessen.

Major Islamic Holidays

The rhythms of Islamic practice are tied to the lunar calendar, so the Muslim calendar begins around 11 days earlier than the preceding year. Dates are approximate as they rely on the sighting of the new moon.

HOLIDAY	2016	2017	2018
Moulid an-Nabi	12 Dec	1 Dec	20 Nov
Ramadan begins	6 Jun	27 May	16 May
Eid al-Fitr	5 Jul	25 Jun	14 Jun
Eid al-Adhar	11 Sep	1 Sep	21 Aug
Islamic New Year	2 Oct	21 Sep	10 Sep

Telephone
☑ **Top Tip** For within-country calls always dial the local four-digit area code.

➡ To call Morocco dial the country code 📞212.

➡ To phone another country from Morocco dial 📞00 followed by the country code.

➡ Moroccan landline numbers start with 📞05.

➡ Mobile phone numbers all begin with 📞06.

Mobile Phones
➡ If you have an unlocked mobile phone you can buy a prepaid mobile SIM card (around Dh50 with credit). Take your passport when purchasing.

➡ Newsstands and grocery stores sell scratch cards for topping up your credit.

Toilets
➡ Public toilets, and toilets in cafes and restaurants, often have no toilet paper (*papier hygiénique*) so keep a supply with you.

➡ Don't throw the paper into the toilet as the plumbing is often dodgy; instead discard it in the bin provided.

Tourist Information
☑ **Top Tip** Most hotels and riads can provide free maps of the city.

➡ The **Office National Marocain du Tourisme** (ONMT; 📞0524 43 61 79; Pl Abdel Moumen ben Ali) in Guéliz is the main tourist office. It provides pamphlets, but not much actual information.

Travellers with Disabilities
Marrakesh has few facilities for the disabled, but is not necessarily out of bounds for travellers with a physical disability and a sense of adventure. Some factors to be aware of:

➡ Narrow medina streets and rutted pavements can make mobility challenging.

➡ Only a handful of top-end hotels have rooms designed for the disabled.

➡ Booking ground-floor rooms is essential as few hotels have lifts.

➡ Vision- or hearing-impaired travellers are poorly catered for. Hearing loops, Braille signs and talking pedestrian crossings are nonexistent.

Visas
➡ Most visitors do not require a visa to visit Morocco and are allowed to remain in the country for 90 days.

➡ Your passport must be valid for at least six months beyond your date of entry.

➡ Further information is available from the **Moroccan Ministry of Foreign Affairs and Cooperation** (www.diplomatie.ma/en).

Language

The official language in Morocco is Arabic, which is used throughout the country. Berber is spoken in the Rif and Atlas Mountains. Most Berbers also speak at least some Arabic. French is still regularly used in the cities.

To enhance your trip with a phrasebook, visit **lonelyplanet.com**. Lonely Planet iPhone phrasebooks are available through the Apple App store.

MOROCCAN ARABIC

Moroccan Arabic (Darija) is a variety of Modern Standard Arabic (MSA), but is so different from it in many respects as to be virtually like another language. This is the everyday spoken language you'll hear when in Morocco. Here, we've represented the Arabic phrases with the Roman alphabet using a simplified pronunciation system.

Basics

Hello.	es salaam alaykum (polite)
	wa alaykum salaam (reponse)
Goodbye.	bessalama/m'a ssalama
Please.	'afak/'afik/'afakum (said to m/f/pl)
Thank you.	shukran
You're welcome.	la shukran 'la wejb
Excuse me.	smeh leeya
Yes./No.	eeyeh/la
How are you?	keef halek?
Fine, thank you.	bekheer, lhamdoo llaah

Eating & Drinking

A table for..., please.
tabla dyal... 'afak

Can I see the menu, please?
nazar na'raf lmaakla lli 'andkum?

What do you recommend?
shnoo tansaani nakul?

I'll try what she/he is having.
gha nzharrab shnoo kaatakul hiyya/huwwa

I'm a vegetarian.
makanakoolsh llehem

Shopping

I'd like to buy...	bgheet nshree...
I'm only looking.	gheer kanshoof
Can I look at it?	wakhkha nshoofha?
How much is it?	bshhal?

Emergencies

Help!	'teqnee!
Go away!	seer fhalek!
I'm lost.	tweddert
Thief!	sheffar!
I've been robbed.	tsreqt
Call the police!	'ayyet 'la lbùlees!
Call a doctor!	'ayyet 'la shee tbeeb!
There's been an accident!	uq'at kseeda!
Where's the toilet?	feen kayn lbeet lma?
I'm sick.	ana mreed
I'm allergic to (penicillin).	'andee lhasaseeya m'a (lbeenseleen)

Time & Numbers

What time is it?	*shal fessa'a?*
yesterday	*lbareh*
today	*lyoom*
tomorrow	*ghedda*
morning	*fessbah*
afternoon	*fel'sheeya*
evening	*'sheeya*
day	*nhar*
week	*l'usbu'*
month	*shshhar*
year	*l'am*

Transport & Directions

I'd like a ... ticket.	*'afak bgheet wahed lwarka l ddar lbayda...*
Where is the ...?	*feen kayn ...?*
airport	*mataar*
bus station	*mhetta dyal ttobeesat*
bus stop	*blasa dyal ttobeesat*
ticket office	*maktab lwerqa*
train station	*lagaar*
What's the fare?	*shhal taman lwarka?*

Please tell me when we get to ...
'afak eela wselna l ... goolhaleeya

Please wait for me.
tsennanee 'afak

Stop here, please.
wqef henna 'afak

BERBER

There are three main dialects among Berber speakers, which in a certain sense also serve as loose lines of ethnic demarcation. The following phrases are a selection from the Tashelhit dialect, the one visitors are likely to find most useful.

Basics

Hello.	*la bes darik/darim (m/f)*
Goodbye.	*akayaoon arbee*
Please.	*barakalaufik*
Thank you.	*barakalaufik*
Yes.	*yah*
No.	*oho*
Excuse me.	*samhiy*

Practicalities

food	*teeremt*
somewhere to sleep	*kra lblast mahengane*
water	*arman*
Do you have...?	*ees daroon ...?*
How much is it?	*minshk aysker?*
I want to go to...	*addowghs...*
Where is (the)...?	*mani gheela...?*
straight	*neeshan*
to the left	*fozelmad*
to the right	*fofasee*
mountain	*adrar*
river	*aseef*
yesterday	*eedgam*
today	*(zig sbah) rass*
tomorrow	*(ghasad) aska*

Behind the Scenes

Send Us Your Feedback

We love to hear from travellers – your comments help make our books better. We read every word, and we guarantee that your feedback goes straight to the authors. Visit **lonelyplanet.com/contact** to submit your updates and suggestions.

Note: We may edit, reproduce and incorporate your comments in Lonely Planet products such as guidebooks, websites and digital products, so let us know if you don't want your comments reproduced or your name acknowledged. For a copy of our privacy policy visit lonelyplanet.com/privacy.

Our Readers

Many thanks to travellers Joyce Thehu and Adam Wood who used the last edition and wrote to us with helpful hints, useful advice and interesting anecdotes.

Jessica's Thanks

Huge thanks to all the Marrakshis who always make coming to Marrakesh such a pleasure. Big thanks to Youssef and Amanda, and Gemma van de Burgt. In particular, thanks to Youssef, Fatima, Hassan, Amine and Ahmed for sharing their slice of Marrakesh with me.

Acknowledgments

Cover photograph: Souq in Marrakesh, Morocco; Art Kowalsky/Alamy.

This Book

This 3rd edition of Lonely Planet's *Pocket Marrakesh* guidebook was researched and written by Jessica Lee. This guidebook was produced by the following:

Destination Editor
Helen Elfer

Product Editor
Anne Mason

Assisting Editors Judith Bamber, Kate Mathews, Charlotte Orr

Regional Senior Cartographer Corey Hutchison

Book Designer
Wibowo Rusli

Cover Researcher
Naomi Parker

Thanks to Anna Harris, Elizabeth Jones, Kate Kiely, Claire Naylor, Karyn Noble, Katie O'Connell, Alison Ridgway

Index

See also separate subindexes for:

🗙 **Eating p157**

🍷 **Drinking p157**

🛍 **Shopping p158**

⊗ Eating

⊕ Drinking